Growth Rate of Plymouth White Rock Chickens
Chicken Breeds Book 50

by H.H. Mitchell

with an introduction by Jackson Chambers

Introduction

I am pleased to present yet another title in the "Chicken Breeds" series.

This volume is entitled "Growth of White Plymouth Rock Chickens" and was authored by H.H. Mitchell in 1926.

The work is in the Public Domain and is re-printed here in accordance with Federal Laws.

Though this work is a century old it contains much information on poultry that is still pertinent today.

As with all reprinted books of this age that are intended to perfectly reproduce the original edition, considerable pains and effort had to be undertaken to correct fading and sometimes outright damage to existing proofs of this title. At times, this task is quite monumental, requiring an almost total "rebuilding" of some pages from digital proofs of multiple copies. Despite this, imperfections still sometimes exist in the final proof and may detract from the visual appearance of the text.

I hope you enjoy reading this book as much as I enjoyed making it available to readers again.

Jackson Chambers

THE GROWTH OF WHITE PLYMOUTH ROCK CHICKENS

By H. H. Mitchell, L. E. Card, and T. S. Hamilton[a]

The rate and manner in which a given species of animal grows, besides being of great physiological importance, must form the basis for any estimation of the nutrient requirements for that species. It is also important that the practical animal husbandman know something of the normal growth of the animals which he is raising, in order that he may judge the success of his own feeding operations.

The most scientific method of estimating the food requirements of any species of animal for growth is undoubtedly the system developed by Armsby relative to the energy requirements. According to this system an estimate of the amount of energy that animals need at different stages of growth must be based upon reliable information relating to three distinct points: first, the maintenance requirement of the animals at different stages of growth; second, the normal rate of increase in body weight during the growing period; and third, the composition of the gains put on at different ages. Furthermore, in order to make practical use of this information in the formulation of feeding standards for growth, it is necessary to know the extent of the utilization of food energy by growing animals at different ages. This system has been developed by Armsby only in connection with energy requirements and the energy values of feeds. There is every reason to suppose, however, that the system could be extended to include other nutrients such as protein and mineral matter, by obtaining for each nutrient information analogous to that just indicated with reference to energy.

The production of meat by growing animals is most commonly measured simply by the increase in weight. However, the increase in weight at different ages is known to vary widely in composition. For example, a pound of protoplasm such as a young animal would put on during growth has an energy value of about 500 calories and a protein content of approximately 20 percent. As the age of the animal increases, the water content of its gains decreases and the nature of the solid matter changes progressively, due to an increasing proportion of fat. In the last stages of fattening, a pound increase in weight may have an energy value of 4,000 calories, and may contain only a mere

[a]H. H. Mitchell, Chief in Animal Nutrition; L. E. Card, Chief in Poultry Husbandry; T. S. Hamilton, Associate in Animal Nutrition.

trace of protein. It is quite evident that as this change in composition of gains takes place the food required to produce these gains will increase in amount and change progressively in quality.

Among practical livestock men it may not be generally realized that the composition of gains put on by meat animals varies as widely as this. Even when it is realized that such differences do occur, little practical use can be made of this knowledge since precise information is not available regarding the composition of the gains which animals put on at different ages.

In dairy production it is well known that the productive capacity of a cow is measured not only by the amount of milk she will produce but also by its composition. Since in this case the product can be so readily removed from the animal and submitted to analysis, many thousands of analyses of milk of different grades have been made with various purposes in view, and have been reported in the literature of the subject. At the present time any thorogoing feeding standard for milk production considers not only the amount of milk produced but also its composition, particularly in energy or total nutrients. Nevertheless, the need for considering the composition of the product in milk production is not so urgent as in meat production, because of the narrower range in the composition of milk as compared with the composition of gains put on by growing and fattening animals. A pound of milk testing 2.5 percent fat, for example, has an energy value of a little over half that of a pound of milk testing 7 percent fat, while a pound of gain put on by a young animal may have an energy value of only one-eighth that of a pound of gain put on by an animal in the last stages of fattening.

The most efficient method for determining the composition of the gains of growing animals is to slaughter animals at different ages and weights and submit their carcasses to a careful chemical examination. From such data the composition of gains between two different weights may be computed by assuming that the animals slaughtered at the higher weight had the same composition at the lower weight as the animals actually killed at that weight. While a considerable number of analyses of the different farm animals at different ages and weights may be found in the literature, the number is still insufficient in many cases to form the basis of a reliable feeding standard. For example, in arriving at his estimate of the energy requirements of growing pigs, Armsby has sought for information concerning the energy content of a pound increase in weight put on by pigs at birth and at an age when growth may be assumed to have been practically complete. The change in composition between these two ages is then assumed to vary in a linear fashion with age. While the experimental information on the composition of the early gains is fairly satisfactory, the information relative to the energy value of gains put on at 18 to 24 months of age consisted of determinations by Soxlet on two pigs 16.5 months of age. One value was 1,401 calories per pound, the other was 2,485 calories per pound. Since the latter value was more consistent with similar data on other animals, it was chosen in preference to the former, but it is evident that much more complete information on this point should be obtained.

No information is available in the literature from which the composition of gains put on by growing poultry may be computed. Very little is known of the maintenance requirement of poultry or of the difference in maintenance requirement between the different sexes. The extent to which poultry utilize the energy of their feeds is also practically unknown, so that the formulation of a scientific estimate of the food requirements of growing chickens is impossible at the present time. The experiment reported in this bulletin is the first of a series of investigations that is being undertaken by the Nutrition and Poultry Divisions of the Illinois Agricultural Experiment Station to obtain information upon which feeding standards for poultry may be based.

DESCRIPTION OF THE EXPERIMENT

The object of the experiment reported in this bulletin was to investigate the growth of White Plymouth Rock chickens by measuring the increase of size of the entire bird and of individual organs for pullets, cockerels, and capons, and by determining the composition of the gains in weight put on at different ages.

A flock of approximately 1,000 White Plymouth Rock chicks hatched March 28, 1923, was used in this investigation. They were range-reared on the colony house plan at the poultry farm, and were fed the standard ration used at this Station for growing birds. Individual weights of the birds were taken every two weeks. When the flock reached an average weight of about 1.5 pounds, the cockerels and pullets were separated and approximately half the cockerels were caponized. From this time on they were fed in three groups—pullets, cockerels, and capons.

Groups of birds were removed according to weight rather than age, for measurement, slaughter, and analysis. Five chicks were selected from the entire flock at weights of .5 pound, 1 pound, and 1.5 pounds, these selections including only cockerels in so far as the sex could be distinguished. To determine whether the measurements and composition of the birds were greatly affected by age, when killed at the same weight, two groups of 5 chicks each, differing by two weeks in age, were slaughtered at the 1-pound weight.

At the 2-pound weight two groups of 5 birds each were selected for slaughter, one consisting of 5 pullets and the other of 5 cockerels.

From this weight on, the selections of birds were made at intervals of 1 pound. Starting with a weight of 3 pounds, 5 pullets, 5 cockerels, and 5 capons were selected for measurement and slaughter. At 1-pound intervals thereafter the growth of pullets was studied up to a weight of 5 pounds, and the growth of cockerels and capons up to a weight of 7 pounds.

The following measurements were made on all birds removed for slaughter:

1. Depth from front end of keel bone to back
2. Depth from rear end of keel bone to back
3. Length from rump to tip of beak
4. Length from rump to shoulder
5. Circumference of trunk just behind wings
6. Length of shank
7. Length of middle toe
8. Length of drumstick
9. Length of keel bone
10. Breadth from hip to hip

The birds were then killed, bled, and dry picked. The skins were removed and their areas determined. The carcasses were then cut up and fresh weights of the following portions were taken:

1. Blood	13. Pancreas
2. Feathers	14. Spleen
3. Head	15. Lungs
4. Shanks and feet	16. Testicles (in cockerels)
5. Skin	17. Gullet and proventriculus
6. Neck	18. Gizzard
7. Legs above hock	19. Intestinal tract
8. Wings	20. Contents of gizzard
9. Torso	21. Contents of intestinal tract
10. Heart	22. Total bones in dressed carcass
11. Liver	23. Total flesh in dressed carcass
12. Kidneys[a]	

The length of the intestinal tract in each bird was also measured.

For each group of 5 birds the following three composite samples were made up for analysis:

1. All bones, except those in head, shanks, and feet
2. Flesh, heart, liver, and gizzard
3. Offal, including the blood, feathers, head, shanks and feet, skin, and all viscera not included in the second sample

Each of these three samples was ground fresh, preserved with exactly 1 percent of thymol (a correction for which was made in reporting the analyses), and analyzed in a fresh condition for moisture, nitrogen, ether extract, and ash. The gross energy of each sample was directly determined in the bomb calorimeter.

---

[a]The kidneys were not weighed in the .5-pound chicks.

EXPERIMENTAL RESULTS

The flock of White Plymouth Rock chickens from which birds were taken for measurement and analysis was weighed at bi-weekly intervals. The weights thus obtained are compiled in Table 1. The weight of 46 grams given as the hatching weight of the chicks is actually the weight of the chicks at two days of age. The birds were obtained from a commercial hatchery and were weighed immediately

TABLE 1.—BIWEEKLY WEIGHTS OF THE WHITE PLYMOUTH ROCK CHICKENS USED IN THIS STUDY

Age	Cockerels			Pullets			Capons		
	Number of birds	Average weight	Biweekly increase in weight	Number of birds	Average weight	Biweekly increase in weight	Number of birds	Average weight	Biweekly increase in weight
wks.		gms.	gms.		gms.	gms.		gms.	gms.
0	...	46	....	...	46	...	...	.....	...
2	400	87	41	507	85	39	...	.....	...
4	401	178	91	502	163	78	...	.....	...
6	401	308	130	493	280	117	...	.....	...
8	399	477	169	472	416	136	...	.....	...
10	391[a]	605	128	420	535	119	...	.....	...
12	184	716	111	384	602	67	150	675	70
14	178	907	191	363	752	150	135	892	217
16	170	1 150	243	353	919	167	139	1 095	210
18	163	1 229	79	322	1 036	117	129	1 271	176
20	152	1 347	118	312	1 140	104	129	1 379	108
22	145	1 557	210	293	1 285	145	119	1 658	279
24	135	1 636	79	281	1 403	118	108	1 849	191
26	118	1 756	120	267	1 533	130	113	1 899	50
28	116	1 962	206	247	1 647	114	74	2 206	307
30	112	2 135	173	230	1 734	89	77	2 330	124
32	116	2 062	−73	223	1 774	40	74	2 371	41
34	93	2 515	453	200	2 025	251	67	2 449	78
36	69	2 536	21	186	2 005	−20	43	2 385	−64
38	70	2 623	87	...	.....	...	39	2 497	112
40	67	2 798	175	...	.....	...	39	2 587	90
42	64	2 744	−54	...	.....	...	42	2 516	−71
44	62	2 804	60	...	.....	...	37	2 679	163
46	46	2 778	−26	...	.....	...	29	2 759	80

[a]Approximately half the cockerels were caponized at this time.

on arrival at Urbana. The decrease in numbers of birds indicated in the table was due not only to mortality, but also to the fact that birds were removed from this flock at various times for purposes other than those of this experiment.

A comparison of the growth rate of these White Plymouth Rock chickens with that recorded by Philips[2] shows that the growth obtained in this experiment was considerably slower and less sustained than that obtained at Purdue. In addition to the fact that these chicks appear to have come from a rather small strain of White Plymouth Rocks, it

TABLE 2.—AVERAGE BODY MEASUREMENTS OF WHITE PLYMOUTH ROCK COCKERELS AT DIFFERENT WEIGHTS: EACH FIGURE IS AN AVERAGE FOR FIVE BIRDS

(All measurements are in centimeters)

Approximate slaughter weight	0.5 lb.	1 lb.	1.5 lbs.	2 lbs.	3 lbs.	4 lbs.	5 lbs.	6 lbs.	7 lbs.
Age in days	29	43–57	71	103	117	169	177	250	324
Live weight in grams	232	449	673	993	1 361	1 786	2 236	2 583	3 253
Depth at front end of keel	5.3	7.0	8.5	9.7	10.9	12.5	13.1	13.4	13.6
Depth at rear end of keel	5.5	7.5	8.7	9.1	10.5	11.2	11.7	12.6	13.8
Length of keel	5.0	6.7	8.0	9.3	10.3	11.7	12.2	13.1	13.9
Length of drumstick	7.0	9.2	11.2	13.6	15.2	17.5	18.4	18.3	18.4
Length of shank	5.3	6.9	8.4	10.6	11.4	13.0	13.8	13.6	13.6
Length of middle toe	4.4	5.5	6.4	7.8	8.1	8.2	9.0	8.5	9.0
Rump to shoulder	(9.1)[a]	11.8	13.8	16.7	18.3	19.8	21.5	21.8	22.4
Length over all	20.0	25.0	29.0	36.0	40.0	44.0	45.0	48.0	47.0
Mid-circumference	14.0	19.0	21.0	26.0	29.0	32.0	35.0	37.0	38.0
Breadth at hips	4.1	5.2	5.8	6.7	7.5	8.8	9.1	9.6	10.5

[a]This measurement was not made on the 0.5-pound chicks of this experiment; the value given was obtained from a number of birds of the same weight from another flock of White Plymouth Rock birds the following year.

should be pointed out that the environment under which they were reared was not ideal. The range area in use contained no natural shade and artificial straw shelters had to be constructed. The lack of shade probably was partly responsible for the rather slow rate of growth obtained.

From two weeks of age on the cockerels increased in weight at a more rapid rate than the pullets (Table 1). No clear difference in growth is apparent between cockerels and capons, except for a slightly more rapid growth of the capons from the 18th to the 32d week.

The biweekly increases in weight exhibit what might be called a cyclic tendency, it will be noted from Table 1. The authors hesitate to attach much significance to these cycles. While there is a tendency to interpret such changes in the rate of growth as indicating "cycles of growth," such an interpretation fails to consider important environmental factors. The weather, particularly, may exhibit periodic variations and these very probably exert a pronounced effect on the growth of the animals. The discussion of this point will be resumed in a later section of the bulletin.

INCREASE IN BODY MEASUREMENTS WITH AGE

The average body measurements of the several groups of birds removed at different weights are given in Tables 2, 3, and 4. These

TABLE 3.—AVERAGE BODY MEASUREMENTS OF WHITE PLYMOUTH ROCK PULLETS AT DIFFERENT WEIGHTS: EACH FIGURE IS AN AVERAGE OF FIVE BIRDS
(All measurements are in centimeters)

Approximate slaughter weight	2 lbs.	3 lbs.	4 lbs.	5 lbs.
Age in days	73	94	189	219
Live weight in grams	961	1 342	1 842	2 340
Depth at front end of keel	9.3	10.7	11.6	12.4
Depth at rear end of keel	9.0	10.1	11.1	12.5
Length of keel	8.9	10.3	11.9	12.7
Length of drumstick	13.0	15.0	15.2	15.8
Length of shank	10.0	11.1	10.9	11.6
Length of middle toe	7.0	7.5	7.1	7.6
Rump to shoulder	16.2	18.0	18.8	19.5
Length over all	35.0	39.0	40.0	41.0
Mid-circumference	25.0	29.0	33.0	36.0
Breath at hips	6.4	7.8	8.1	8.9

tables also include the average live weight in grams and the age in days. Each group of birds includes 5 individuals, except the group removed at approximately 1 pound in weight, which includes two lots of birds measured at dates two weeks apart. The measurements for these two lots at the same weight were so nearly the same that they have been averaged together.[a]

The change in size of the birds as indicated by these measurements may be studied to best advantage probably by expressing the average measurements at increasing weights in percentage of the corresponding measurement of the .5-pound chicks. This has been done for the cockerels as shown in Table 5, which also includes values relating to body surface. Practically all of the measurements taken on these birds increased in approximately the same proportion when referred to the measurements of the .5-pound chicks. Thus, for all of the measurements except the length of middle toe the 7-pound cock-

TABLE 4.—AVERAGE BODY MEASUREMENTS OF WHITE PLYMOUTH ROCK CAPONS AT DIFFERENT WEIGHTS: EACH FIGURE IS AN AVERAGE OF FIVE BIRDS
(All measurements are in centimeters)

Approximate slaughter weight	3 lbs.	4 lbs.	5 lbs.	6 lbs.	7 lbs.
Age in days	88	170	180	215	240
Live weight in grams	1 375	1 702	2 285	2 684	3 188
Depth at front end of keel	11.0	12.3	13.2	13.2	13.4
Depth at rear end of keel	10.2	10.8	12.3	12.2	13.4
Length of keel	9.7	11.1	12.1	13.0	13.5
Length of drumstick	15.3	17.1	18.4	18.5	18.2
Length of shank	11.7	12.6	13.8	13.5	13.4
Length of middle toe	7.9	8.0	8.7	8.4	8.7
Rump to shoulder	17.8	19.8	20.6	22.2	21.9
Length over all	39.0	45.0	44.0	47.0	46.0
Mid-circumference	29.0	30.0	35.0	37.0	40.0
Breadth at hips	7.8	8.4	8.7	9.4	9.8

erels were approximately 2.5 times as large as the .5-pound. This can be interpreted to mean that the conformation of the birds did not change materially during the whole course of growth from .5 pound to 7 pounds in weight. The body weight itself, of course, increased much more rapidly when computed in this way than did the body measurements, while the body surface, as would be expected, increased much

[a]The average measurements of these two groups of birds removed at a weight of approximately 1 pound, but at an interval of two weeks, were as follows:

(Body measurements in centimeters)

Age days	Body weight gms.	Body surface sq. cms.	Depth at front	Depth at rear	Length of keel	Length of drumstick	Length of shank	Length of middle	Breadth at hips	Rump to tip of beak	Circumference	Rump to shoulder
43	446	518	7.0	7.5	6.7	9.1	6.9	5.5	5.2	25.1	19.1	11.8
57	452	511	7.1	7.5	6.8	9.4	6.9	5.6	5.2	25.7	19.4	11.9

less rapidly than did the body weight. The increase in size of the pullets and capons may be studied by a slightly different method, as exemplified in Tables 6 and 7. In these tables the body measurements of pullets and capons of different weights have been expressed as percentages of the corresponding measurements of cockerels of the same weight. In this way, differences in the conformation of these two groups of birds as compared to the cockerels have been brought out.

TABLE 5.—RELATIVE INCREASE IN BODY WEIGHT, BODY SURFACE, AND BODY MEASUREMENTS OF WHITE PLYMOUTH ROCK COCKERELS DURING GROWTH

Approximate slaughter weight	0.5 lb.	1 lb.	1.5 lbs.	2 lbs.	3 lbs.	4 lbs.	5 lbs.	6 lbs.	7 lbs.
BODY WEIGHT..........	100	194	290	428	587	769	964	1 113	1 402
BODY SURFACE..........	100	193	279	369	452	549	659	731	814
BODY MEASUREMENTS									
Depth at front end of keel...............	100	132	160	183	206	236	247	253	257
Depth at rear end of keel...............	100	136	158	165	191	204	213	229	251
Length of keel.........	100	134	160	186	206	234	244	262	278
Length of drumstick...	100	131	160	194	217	250	263	261	263
Length of shank.......	100	130	158	200	215	245	260	257	257
Length of middle toe..	100	125	145	177	184	186	205	193	205
Rump to shoulder.....	100	130	152	184	201	218	236	240	242
Length over all.......	100	130	148	184	204	224	230	245	246
Mid-circumference....	100	134	150	179	203	224	245	259	266
Breadth at hips.......	100	127	141	163	183	215	222	234	256

TABLE 6.—AVERAGE BODY MEASUREMENTS OF WHITE PLYMOUTH ROCK PULLETS AT DIFFERENT WEIGHTS, EXPRESSED AS PERCENTAGES OF THE CORRESPONDING MEASUREMENTS OF COCKERELS

Approximate slaughter weight	2 lbs.	3 lbs.	4 lbs.	5 lbs.
Age in days....................................	73	94	189	219
Live weight in grams...........................	961	1 342	1 842	2 340
Depth at front end of keel......................	96	98	93	95
Depth at rear end of keel......................	99	96	99	107
Length of keel.................................	97	100	102	104
Length of drumstick...........................	96	99	87	86
Length of shank...............................	94	97	84	84
Length of middle toe...........................	90	93	87	84
Rump to shoulder..............................	97	98	95	91
Mid-circumference.............................	98	97	91	91
Breadth at hips................................	96	104	92	98

The pullets at any weight were, in general, smaller in external measurement than the cockerels of like weight (Table 6). The only measurement remaining approximately the same in the two sexes is the length of keel. The leg measurements of the pullets in particular were appreciably smaller than those of the cockerels, especially after the weight of 3 pounds was reached.

A similar comparison of capons and cockerels is made in Table 7. Altho most of the measurements on the capons were slightly less than the corresponding measurements on cockerels of similar weight, no very distinct differences are evident. Castration does not appreciably affect the body conformation of White Plymouth Rock chickens.

TABLE 7.—AVERAGE BODY MEASUREMENTS OF WHITE PLYMOUTH ROCK CAPONS AT DIFFERENT WEIGHTS, EXPRESSED AS PERCENTAGES OF THE CORRESPONDING MEASUREMENTS OF COCKERELS

Approximate slaughter weight	3 lbs.	4 lbs.	5 lbs.	6 lbs.	7 lbs.
Age in days	88	170	180	215	240
Live weight in grams	1 375	1 702	2 285	2 684	3 188
Depth at front end of keel	101	98	101	99	99
Depth at rear end of keel	97	96	105	97	97
Length of keel	94	95	99	99	97
Length of drumstick	101	98	100	101	99
Length of shank	103	97	100	99	99
Length of middle toe	98	98	97	99	97
Rump to shoulder	97	100	96	102	100
Length over all	97	102	98	98	98
Mid-circumference	100	94	100	100	105
Breadth at hips	104	95	96	98	93

SURFACE AREA OF THE BIRDS AT DIFFERENT AGES

One of the objects of this investigation was to determine the surface area of the birds at different ages and weights, for the purpose of deriving a formula by which the area of a bird may be computed from certain measurements that can be taken readily on the live bird. The idea in mind was to use such a formula in later work in determining the intensity of the basal heat production per unit of body surface. Therefore, after the birds were killed and picked, the skin was removed and cut up into sections that would flatten out evenly. The sections were then stretched on paper, pinned down, and outlined in pencil. It was very soon found that the skins were quite elastic, so that the tension of the stretched skin could be varied considerably. In all of this work, therefore, the skins were stretched about as much as possible, and in order to determine the error resulting from differences in the tension applied, each skin was stretched independently by two men and thus outlined twice. The area of each outline was then measured with a planimeter.

The average results of these determinations are given in Table 8. There is also included, for each group of 5 birds, the average percent-

TABLE 8.—AVERAGE SKIN AREAS OF WHITE PLYMOUTH ROCK CHICKENS KILLED AT DIFFERENT WEIGHTS: EACH FIGURE IS AN AVERAGE OF FIVE BIRDS

(All areas are in square centimeters)

Approximate slaughter weight	0.5 lb.	1 lb.	1.5 lbs.	2 lbs.	3 lbs.	4 lbs.	5 lbs.	6 lbs.	7 lbs.
COCKERELS									
Average skin area	267	514[a]	744	986	1 206	1 467	1 760	1 952	2 173
Average percentage difference between duplicate determinations	7.4	6.3	6.1	5.7	10.7	7.8	7.3	6.5	3.9
PULLETS									
Average skin area	……	……	……	920	1 214	1 574	1 675	……	……
Average percentage difference between duplicate determinations	……	……	……	6.2	9.3	8.1	4.1	……	……
CAPONS									
Average skin area	……	……	……	……	1 216	1 683	1 744	1 880	2 096
Average percentage difference between duplicate determinations	……	……	……	……	3.7	5.3	4.0	9.8	12.3

[a]Average of 10 birds.

age difference between duplicate determinations. It is evident that the error in this direct determination of skin area is considerable and varies widely. It also appears that, except for the 4-pound birds, the skin area of cockerels, pullets, and capons of similar weight was quite similar. At least no constant differences between the three groups of birds are revealed.

The first attempt to estimate the skin area of the cockerels, for which the most complete series of determinations was available, is shown in Table 9. Since the Meeh formula is the simplest formula relating surface to weight, and hence the most practicable when a reasonable degree of accuracy can be realized by its use, it was applied first to the nine groups of cockerels. The average value for k from these nine average determinations was 9.55. A comparison of the actual skin areas with the estimated skin areas, using the formula $S = 9.55\,W^{2/3}$, is given in the upper part of the table. The formula evidently gives a very poor determination for the .5-pound chicks, and an indifferent determination for the 1-, 5-, and 6-pound birds.

If the .5-pound chicks are disregarded in the determination of the Meeh constant, the average value of this constant becomes 9.85 instead of 9.55. Using the latter constant in estimating the skin area of the last eight groups of birds, the values given in the lower half of Table 9 are obtained. While the estimated areas for the 5- and 6-pound birds are less in error than the estimates by the other formula, the estimate for the 1-pound chicks is considerably less accurate. However, the Meeh formula can be considered to apply with considerable accuracy to birds weighing more than 1 pound, and if the constant were still further raised, even a better fit would be obtained above this weight. The success of the Meeh formula as applied to the estimation of the surface area of White Plymouth Rock chicks is to be expected from the fact illustrated in Table 5 that the conformation of this breed of birds is not greatly affected by size.

In attempting to improve the Meeh formula for chickens, the successful experience of investigators, working with other animals, in introducing a linear body measurement into the formula, was considered. The measurement most frequently used with the weight in defining the conformation of an animal is a measurement relating to the body length. Thus, Du Bois' formula for computing the surface area of human beings introduces the height measurement, while the formulas of Hogan and Skouby[3] for the determination of the surface area of cattle and swine introduce a body length formula, that is, the length from the point of the withers to the end of the ischium, or to the root of the tail. The corresponding measurement on a chicken might be taken as the total body length from beak to rump. But in the experience of the authors, this length is difficult to take accurately,

TABLE 9.—ESTIMATION OF THE SKIN AREA OF WHITE PLYMOUTH ROCK CHICKENS BY MEANS OF THE MEEH FORMULA

(All areas are in square centimeters)

Approximate slaughter weight	0.5 lb.	1 lb.	1.5 lbs.	2 lbs.	3 lbs.	4 lbs.	5 lbs.	6 lbs.	7 lbs.
COCKERELS									
With k = 9.55									
Actual skin area	267	514	744	986	1 206	1 467	1 760	1 952	2 173
Estimated skin area	361	560	733	951	1 173	1 406	1 633	1 778	2 097
Error in percentage	+26.0	+9.0	−1.5	−3.5	−2.7	−4.1	−7.1	−8.2	−3.5
With k = 9.85									
Estimated skin area	.....	577	756	980	1 210	1 450	1 684	1 854	2 163
Error in percentage	.....	+12.3	+1.6	−0.6	+0.3	−1.2	−4.3	−5.3	−0.6
PULLETS									
With k = 9.85									
Actual skin area	.....	.....	.....	920	1 214	1 574	1 675	.....	.....
Estimated skin area	.....	.....	.....	959	1 199	1 480	1 736	.....	.....
Error in percentage	.....	.....	.....	+4.2	−1.2	−6.0	+3.7	.....	.....
CAPONS									
With k = 9.85									
Actual skin area	.....	.....	.....	.....	1 216	1 683	1 744	1 880	2 096
Estimated skin area	.....	.....	.....	.....	1 218	1 405	1 709	1 902	2 133
Error in percentage	.....	.....	.....	.....	−0.2	−16.5	−2.0	+1.2	+1.8

because the distance obtained depends so much on the tension used in stretching out the bird. An alternative measurement which could be obtained with great accuracy was the shoulder-to-rump measurement. However, a formula involving both weight and rump-to-shoulder distance that would apply satisfactorily to all nine groups of cockerels could not be found, the error in estimating the area of the .5-pound chicks being almost as great as that resulting from the application of the Meeh formula. If the .5-pound chicks are disregarded, however, the following formula is found to apply satisfactorily to the heavier cockerels: $S = 5.86\,W^{.5}L^{.6}$, in which S is the area in square centimeters, W the body weight in grams, and L the rump-to-shoulder measurement in centimeters.

The estimates made by this formula of the area of the remaining eight groups of cockerels are given in the upper section of Table 10. While this formula gives a better estimate of surface area in these classes than the Meeh formula, the estimate for the 1-pound birds is still appreciably higher than the actual area.

Using the same formula with the same constant in estimating the area of the pullets and capons, satisfactory results were obtained with the exception of the 4-pound birds in each of the groups. For some reason, at present unknown, the observed areas of the 4-pound capons, and to a less extent of the 4-pound pullets, were considerably higher than the areas of the 4-pound cockerels, and were so much greater than the observed areas for the 3-pound pullets and capons that they may be considered as exceptional values, not representative of birds of this size. Since there seemed to be no hope of devising a formula that would take care of these exceptional values any better than the one given above, no further attempt was made to improve upon it.

In attempting to see whether the weight-body-length formula given above for White Plymouth Rock chickens would apply to other breeds of chickens, the weight, the distance from rump to shoulder, and the skin areas of 5 Rhode Island Red hens and of 5 Single Comb White Leghorn hens were determined. The area was then estimated by means of the formula derived from White Plymouth Rock measurements. The results of this test are given in Table 11, from which it is evident that the areas of the Rhode Island Red hens could be estimated with considerable accuracy with this formula, probably just as accurately as they could be measured directly by skinning the birds. For the White Leghorn hens, however, the estimate was always considerably in excess of the actual area. However, by reducing the constant from 5.86 to 5.03, the resulting estimates of skin area were satisfactory. The conformation of Rhode Island Red hens is very similar to that of White Plymouth Rock hens, while the conformation of White Leghorn hens is distinctly different.

TABLE 10.—ESTIMATION OF THE SKIN AREA OF WHITE PLYMOUTH ROCK CHICKENS BY MEANS OF THE
FORMULA $S = 5.86\ W^{.5}\ L^{.6}$

(All areas are in square centimeters)

Approximate slaughter weight	0.5 lb.	1 lb.	1.5 lbs.	2 lbs.	3 lbs.	4 lbs.	5 lbs.	6 lbs.	7 lbs.
COCKERELS									
Actual area	267	514	744	986	1 206	1 467	1 760	1 952	2 173
Estimated area	.....	546	734	1 000	1 181	1 485	1 746	1 892	2 159
Error in percentage	.....	+6.2	−1.3	+1.4	−2.1	+1.2	−0.8	−3.4	−0.7
PULLETS									
Actual area	.....	.....	.....	920	1 214	1 574	1 675	.....	.....
Estimated area	.....	.....	.....	966	1 216	1 462	1 685	.....	.....
Error in percentage	.....	.....	.....	+5.0	+0.2	−7.1	+0.6	.....	.....
CAPONS									
Actual area	.....	.....	.....	.....	1 216	1 683	1 744	1 880	2 096
Estimated area	.....	.....	.....	.....	1 223	1 450	1 721	1 950	2 108
Error in percentage	.....	.....	.....	.....	+0.6	−13.9	−1.3	+3.7	+0.6

TABLE 11.—ESTIMATION OF THE SKIN AREA OF FIVE RHODE ISLAND RED HENS AND OF FIVE WHITE LEGHORN HENS BY MEANS OF THE FORMULA $S = 5.86\ W^{.5} L^{.5}$

(All areas are in square centimeters)

	Hen 1	Hen 2	Hen 3	Hen 4	Hen 5
RHODE ISLAND RED HENS					
Live weight of hen (W), *gms*	3 550	2 515	3 030	2 338	1 957
Rump-to-shoulder measurement (L), *cms*	20.5	18.5	19.3	18.5	17.0
Estimation of area by formula	2 138	1 692	1 905	1 632	1 419
Duplicate determinations of area	2 112	1 697	1 841	1 649	1 392
	2 425	1 699	1 987	1 695	1 469
Error of estimate in percentage	−5.8	−0.4	−0.5	−2.4	−0.9
WHITE LEGHORN HENS					
Live weight of hen (W), *gms*	1 539	1 391	1 805	1 427	1 217
Rump-to-shoulder measurement (L), *cms*	16.8	15.8	15.5	15.7	16.7
Estimation of area by formula	1 232	1 145	1 289	1 155	1 107
Duplicate determinations of area	1 076	985	1 057	967	810
	1 097	1 066	1 124	1 039	988
Error of estimate in percentage	+13.3	+11.6	+18.2	+15.2	+23.1
Estimation by formula $S = 5.03\ W^{.5} L^{.5}$	1 073	983	1 107	992	950
Error of estimate in percentage	−1.3	−4.2	+1.5	−1.0	+5.7

RELATIVE AND ABSOLUTE GROWTH OF THE DIFFERENT PARTS OF THE CARCASS AND VISCERA

The growth of the different parts of the carcass and of the viscera of the groups of cockerels, pullets, and capons is represented by the average values given in Tables 12, 13, and 14. These tables include the average weights for each group of 5 birds. Again the two lots of 1-pound birds have been averaged together, since the difference of two weeks in their ages did not seem to affect the results materially.[a] Most of the viscera and the different parts of the carcass increase continuously with increasing body weight. For cockerels the rapid increase in size of the testicles at about the 6-pound weight clearly indicates the time of sexual maturity. The digestive organs are somewhat exceptional in their growth, since they reach their maximum size before the bird has obtained its complete growth. This is true of all three groups of birds. The weights of the gizzard and of the intestinal tract exclusive of the gizzard reach their maximum when the weight of the bird is 5 or 6 pounds. The weights of the spleen and liver increase but little after this body weight is reached. This attainment of maximum growth of the digestive tract at a time when the body has not ceased growing is also shown by the data in Table 15, relative to the length of the intestinal tract. The maximum length of intestinal tract seems to be reached at a weight of 5 pounds.

Data on the growth of the different parts of the carcass and the different visceral organs, which show for each weight group the percentages of the empty weight of the bird reached by each organ and each part of the carcass, are presented in Tables 16, 17, and 18. The empty weight was obtained by deducting from the average live weight

---

[a]The average weights of the different organs and parts of carcass for the two groups of birds of approximately the same weight (1 pound) but at different ages, were as follows, all weights being given in grams:

Age days	Body weight	Viscera and offal								
		Blood	Feathers	Head	Shanks + feet	Heart	Liver	Kidneys	Pancreas	Spleen
43.....	446	21	18	19	23	3.0	16	—	1.9	0.8
57.....	452	19	16	20	23	2.9	15	4.5	1.7	1.1

Age days	Viscera and offal (cont'd)					Dressed carcass				
	Lungs	Testicles	Intestinal tract minus gizzard	Gizzard	Contents of intestinal tract	Neck	Skin	Legs above hock	Wings	Torso
43.....	2.5	0.2	46	16	30	15	32	74	27	95
57.....	2.7	0.1	39	19	23	16	33	79	27	95

The total bone on the dressed carcass weighed 70 and 75 grams respectively for the two groups of birds, while the total flesh on the dressed carcass weighed 131 and 138 grams respectively.

TABLE 12.—AVERAGE WEIGHTS OF PARTS OF CARCASS OF WHITE PLYMOUTH ROCK COCKERELS KILLED AT DIFFERENT WEIGHTS: EACH FIGURE IS AN AVERAGE OF FIVE BIRDS

(All weights are in grams)

	0.5 lb.	1[b] lb.	1.5 lbs.	2 lbs.	3 lbs.	4 lbs.	5 lbs.	6 lbs.	7 lbs.
Approximate slaughter weight									
Age in days	29	43–57	71	103	117	169	177	250	324
Live weight in grams	232	449	673	993	1 361	1 786	2 236	2 583	3 253
VISCERA AND OFFAL									
Blood	9.1	20	29	46	53	72	95	106	150
Feathers	9.3	17	32	46	83	134	174	204	184
Head	12	19	27	33	43	54	61	71	102
Shanks and feet	11	23	36	56	82	95	113	114	130
Heart	1.7	2.9	3.7	4.6	5.6	7.3	9.3	11.2	21
Liver	7.9	15.5	19.4	22	30	36	45	51	42
Kidneys	....	4.5[c]	5.3	6.2	7.8	8.6	11.4	13.1	12.4
Pancreas	1.1	1.8	2.1	2.9	2.9	3.7	4.9	4.4	5.4
Spleen	0.4	0.9	1.7	1.9	2.7	2.9	4.0	4.0	3.5
Lungs	1.3	2.6	3.3	4.2	6.7	9.1	11.9	11.3	13.7
Testicles	0.1[a]	0.15[d]	0.2	0.3	0.3	1.4	1.4	6.5	33
Intestinal tract exclusive of gizzard	19	43	54	77	83	94	120	132	118
Gizzard	11	17	26	38	47	55	71	68	66
Contents of digestive tract	16	26	36	26	56	61	80	74	71
DRESSED CARCASS									
Neck	8	15	21	38	48	63	73	85	107
Skin	14	33	49	71	91	127	175	190	272
Legs above hock	35	76	121	195	280	381	477	558	793
Wings	14	27	40	62	87	113	127	149	182
Torso	46	95	143	213	305	425	538	663	855
Total bone in carcass (exclusive of head, shanks, and feet)	39	72	109	185	244	330	402	418	510
Total flesh and fat (exclusive of head, shanks, and feet)	54	134	210	323	471	621	796	1 010	1 463

[a]Only 4 of the 5 chicks proved to be cockerels. [b]Averages for 10 birds, 5 being 43 days old and 5, 57 days old. [c]Average of 5 birds only. [d]One of the 10 chicks proved to be a pullet.

of each group of birds the average weight of the contents of the intestinal tract, including the gizzard. For convenience of study, the organs and different parts of the carcass have been arranged into three main groups: first, the offal, which in this tabulation, however, does not include the inedible viscera; second, the visceral organs; and third, the different parts of the dressed carcass. It is interesting to note that the offal parts of the carcass constitute a fairly constant percentage of the empty live weight of the birds at all weights, namely, very close to 19 percent. At the heavier weights there is a slight

TABLE 13.—AVERAGE WEIGHTS OF PARTS OF CARCASS OF WHITE PLYMOUTH ROCK PULLETS KILLED AT DIFFERENT WEIGHTS: EACH FIGURE IS AN AVERAGE OF FIVE BIRDS
(All weights are in grams)

Approximate slaughter weight	2 lbs.	3 lbs.	4 lbs.	5 lbs.
Age in days	73	94	189	219
Live weight in grams	961	1 342	1 842	2 340
VISCERA AND OFFAL				
Blood	34	41	59	79
Feathers	66	108	152	168
Head	28	37	49	53
Shanks and feet	46	61	66	80
Heart	4.5	5.4	8.5	10.1
Liver	23	28	31	43
Kidneys	6.2	8.1	9.8	13.9
Pancreas	2.8	2.9	4.3	4.9
Spleen	2.4	3.0	3.3	4.8
Lungs	4.2	6.6	8.0	8.9
Intestinal tract exclusive of gizzard	65	83	108	128
Gizzard	39	47	60	65
Contents of digestive tract	46	49	55	95
DRESSED CARCASS				
Neck	35	45	52	61
Skin	73	103	164	225
Legs above hock	167	258	344	428
Wings	57	82	97	122
Torso	220	345	524	681
Total bone in carcass (except head, shanks, and feet)	161	224	268	332
Total flesh and fat in carcass (except head, shanks, and feet)	311	497	733	941

tendency for this percentage to decrease. This constancy in percentage weight is particularly apparent for the blood weights. Blood apparently constitutes a consistently higher percentage of the empty weight for the cockerels than for either capons or pullets, the capons ranking next to the cockerels in this respect.

Following an initial increase from the .5-pound to 1-pound chicks, the percentage weight of the total viscera shows a continuous decrease

TABLE 14.—AVERAGE WEIGHTS OF PARTS OF CARCASS OF WHITE PLYMOUTH ROCK CAPONS KILLED AT DIFFERENT WEIGHTS: EACH FIGURE IS AN AVERAGE OF FIVE BIRDS

(All weights are in grams)

Approximate slaughter weight	3 lbs.	4 lbs.	5 lbs.	6 lbs.	7 lbs.
Age in days	88	170	180	215	240
Live weight in grams	1 375	1 702	2 285	2 684	3 188
VISCERA AND OFFAL					
Blood	54	67	96	91	113
Feathers	86	141	178	201	222
Head	40	51	57	60	70
Shanks and feet	77	88	111	129	124
Heart	6.1	6.9	9.1	11.0	13.6
Liver	32	36	49	51	70
Kidneys	8.4	10.2	12.1	14.1	16.2
Pancreas	2.7	3.7	4.9	5.6	5.4
Spleen	2.8	4.1	4.6	5.9	6.4
Lungs	6.8	9.8	11.1	12.8	12.9
Intestinal tract exclusive of gizzard	84	93	133	158	152
Gizzard	47	57	61	74	79
Contents of intestinal tract	60	46	60	85	95
DRESSED CARCASS					
Neck	48	58	69	82	89
Skin	99	136	191	228	272
Legs above hock	267	346	475	528	610
Wings	86	105	131	148	183
Torso	331	405	566	733	969
Total bone in carcass (except head, shanks, and feet)	238	319	391	441	497
Total flesh and fat in carcass (except head, shanks, and feet)	485	559	815	1 019	1 360

TABLE 15.—LENGTH OF INTESTINAL TRACT OF WHITE PLYMOUTH ROCK CHICKENS KILLED AT DIFFERENT WEIGHTS: EACH FIGURE IS AN AVERAGE OF FIVE BIRDS

(All measurements are in centimeters)

Approximate slaughter weight	0.5 lb.	1 lb.	1.5 lbs.	2 lbs.	3 lbs.	4 lbs.	5 lbs.	6 lbs.	7 lbs.
COCKERELS									
Intestines	102	134	142	149	166	176	189	184	174
Ceca (total)	21	26	32	34	35	42	49	45	45
PULLETS									
Intestines	...	...	...	152	151	165	176	...	...
Ceca (total)	...	...	...	42	35	40	48	...	...
CAPONS									
Intestines	...	...	...	...	162	165	190	193	198
Ceca (total)	...	...	...	...	40	38	61	50	48

TABLE 16.—AVERAGE WEIGHTS OF PARTS OF CARCASS OF WHITE PLYMOUTH ROCK COCKERELS KILLED AT DIFFERENT WEIGHTS, EXPRESSED IN PERCENTAGE OF THE EMPTY WEIGHT

	0.5 lb.	1 lb.	1.5 lbs.	2 lbs.	3 lbs.	4 lbs.	5 lbs.	6 lbs.	7 lbs.
Approximate slaughter weight									
Age in days	29	43–57	71	103	117	169	177	250	324
Percentage "fill"	6.8	5.8	5.3	2.6	4.1	3.4	3.6	2.9	2.2
Empty weight in grams	216	423	637	967	1 305	1 725	2 156	2 509	3 182
OFFAL	perct.	perct.	perct.	perct.	perct.	perct.	perct.	perct.	perct.
Feathers	4.3	4.0	5.0	4.8	6.4	7.8	8.1	8.1	5.8
Blood	4.2	4.7	4.6	4.8	4.1	4.2	4.4	4.2	4.7
Head	5.6	4.5	4.2	3.4	3.3	3.1	2.9	2.8	3.2
Shanks and feet	5.1	5.4	5.7	5.8	6.3	5.5	5.2	4.5	4.1
Total offal	19.2	18.7	19.5	18.7	20.0	20.6	20.6	19.7	17.8
VISCERA									
Heart	0.80	0.68	0.58	0.48	0.43	0.42	0.43	0.45	0.66
Liver	3.7	3.7	3.0	2.3	2.3	2.1	2.0	2.0	1.3
Kidneys		1.1	0.83	0.64	0.60	0.50	0.53	0.52	0.39
Pancreas	0.51	0.42	0.33	0.30	0.22	0.21	0.23	0.18	0.17
Spleen	0.19	0.21	0.27	0.20	0.21	0.17	0.19	0.16	0.11
Lungs	0.60	0.58	0.52	0.43	0.51	0.53	0.55	0.45	0.43
Testicles	0.05	0.04	0.03	0.03	0.02	0.09	0.06	0.26	1.04
Digestive tract	13.9	14.2	12.6	11.9	10.0	8.6	7.2	7.9	5.8
Total viscera	19.7	22.1	18.2	16.2	14.3	12.6	12.9	12.0	9.9
DRESSED CARCASS									
Skin	6.5	7.8	7.7	7.3	7.0	7.4	8.1	7.6	8.5
Neck	3.7	3.5	3.3	3.9	3.7	3.7	3.4	3.4	3.4
Legs above hock	16.2	18.0	19.0	20.2	21.5	22.1	22.1	22.2	24.9
Wings	6.5	6.4	6.3	6.4	6.7	6.6	5.9	5.9	5.7
Torso	21.3	22.5	22.4	22.0	23.4	24.6	25.0	26.4	26.9
Total dressed carcass	54.2	58.1	58.7	59.9	62.2	64.3	64.5	65.6	69.4
Total bone in dressed carcass	18.1	17.0	17.1	19.1	18.7	19.1	18.7	16.7	16.0
Total flesh and fat in dressed carcass	25.0	31.7	33.0	33.4	36.1	36.0	36.9	40.2	46.0
Total flesh, fat, and edible viscera[a]	34.5	41.1	41.5	40.7	43.0	42.2	43.3	45.9	50.4

[a]Including heart, liver, gizzard, and kidneys.

with increasing weight of the birds, this being true for all three groups of birds. Jackson[t] and Donaldson[5] have shown that the relative weight of the viscera decreases with increasing body weight in the case of the albino rat, man, and other mammals. This relative decrease is shown for all organs listed except the testicles, and is particularly pronounced for the digestive tract. The decrease is not so marked for the heart, kidneys, and lungs.

Donaldson[6] has shown that the musculature contributes most to the increasing weight of growing mammals. That the same is true for growing fowls is indicated by the tables under discussion. The percentage weight of the total dressed carcass increases slightly but con-

TABLE 17.—AVERAGE WEIGHTS OF PARTS OF CARCASS OF WHITE PLYMOUTH ROCK PULLETS KILLED AT DIFFERENT WEIGHTS, EXPRESSED IN PERCENTAGE OF THE EMPTY WEIGHT

Approximate slaughter weight	2 lbs.	3 lbs.	4 lbs.	5 lbs.
Age in days	73	94	189	219
Percentage "fill"	4.8	3.7	2.6	3.7
Empty weight in grams	915	1 293	1 787	2 245
OFFAL	perct.	perct.	perct.	perct.
Feathers	7.2	8.4	8.5	7.5
Blood	3.7	3.2	3.3	3.5
Head	3.1	2.9	2.7	2.4
Shanks and feet	5.0	4.7	3.7	3.6
Total offal	19.0	19.1	18.2	16.9
VISCERA				
Heart	0.49	0.42	0.48	0.45
Liver	2.5	2.2	1.7	1.9
Kidneys	0.68	0.63	0.55	0.62
Pancreas	0.31	0.22	0.24	0.22
Spleen	0.26	0.23	0.18	0.21
Lungs	0.46	0.51	0.45	0.40
Digestive tract	11.4	10.1	9.4	8.6
Total viscera	16.1	14.2	12.9	12.4
DRESSED CARCASS				
Skin	8.0	8.0	9.2	10.0
Neck	3.8	3.5	2.9	2.7
Legs above hock	18.3	20.0	19.3	19.0
Wings	6.2	6.3	5.4	5.4
Torso	24.0	26.7	29.3	30.2
Total dressed carcass	60.3	64.4	66.1	67.3
Total bone in dressed carcass	17.6	17.3	15.0	14.7
Total flesh and fat in dressed carcass	34.0	38.4	41.0	41.8
Total flesh, fat, and edible viscera[a]	41.9	45.3	47.0	47.6

[a]Including heart, liver, gizzard, and kidneys.

tinuously with increasing weight of body. This increase is particularly marked for the "torso."[a] For the cockerels the relative weight of the

---

[a]"Torso" in this connection refers to the carcass of the bird minus the skin, neck, legs, and wings.

legs above hock also increases steadily with increasing body weight, while for the pullets and capons the percentage weight of the legs above hock is practically constant for all body weights. The percentage weight of the skin also increases, while that for the wings decreases for all three groups of birds.

That the relative increase in dressed carcass relates to the musculature and not to the bones is shown by the percentages at the bottom

TABLE 18.—AVERAGE WEIGHTS OF PARTS OF CARCASS OF WHITE PLYMOUTH ROCK CAPONS KILLED AT DIFFERENT WEIGHTS, EXPRESSED IN PERCENTAGE OF THE EMPTY WEIGHT

Approximate slaughter weight.........	3 lbs.	4 lbs.	5 lbs.	6 lbs.	7 lbs.
Age in days.....................	88	170	180	215	240
Percentage "fill".....................	4.4	2.7	2.6	3.5	3.0
Empty weight in grams................	1 315	1 656	2 225	2 599	3 093
OFFAL	perct.	perct.	perct.	perct.	perct.
Feathers.........................	6.5	8.5	8.0	7.8	7.2
Blood............................	4.1	4.0	4.3	3.5	3.7
Head............................	3.0	3.1	2.6	2.3	2.3
Shanks and feet.....................	5.8	5.4	5.0	5.0	4.0
Total offal........................	19.5	21.0	19.9	18.6	17.1
VISCERA					
Heart............................	0.46	0.42	0.41	0.42	0.44
Liver.............................	2.4	2.2	2.2	1.9	2.3
Kidneys..........................	0.64	0.62	0.54	0.54	0.52
Pancreas.........................	0.21	0.22	0.22	0.22	0.17
Spleen...........................	0.21	0.25	0.21	0.23	0.21
Lungs............................	0.52	0.59	0.50	0.49	0.42
Digestive tract.....................	10.0	9.1	8.7	9.0	7.5
Total viscera......................	14.4	13.3	12.7	12.7	11.5
DRESSED CARCASS					
Skin.............................	7.5	8.2	8.6	8.8	8.8
Neck............................	3.6	3.5	3.1	3.2	2.9
Legs above hock....................	20.3	20.9	21.3	20.4	19.7
Wings............................	6.5	6.3	5.9	5.7	5.9
Torso............................	25.2	24.5	25.4	28.3	31.3
Total dressed carcass................	63.2	64.6	64.4	66.4	68.6
Total bone in dressed carcass...........	18.1	19.3	17.6	17.0	16.1
Total flesh and fat in dressed carcass....	36.9	33.8	36.6	39.3	44.0
Total flesh, fat, and edible viscera[a]......	44.0	40.4	42.4	45.0	49.7

[a]Including heart, liver, gizzard, and kidneys.

of Tables 16, 17, and 18. For all three groups of birds the percentage weight of the bone in the dressed carcass decreases with increasing body weight, while the percentage weight of the total flesh and fat increases. The relative weight of total flesh, fat, and edible viscera (heart, liver, gizzard, and kidneys) also increases with increasing weight of body.

TABLE 19.—RELATIVE INCREASE IN WEIGHT OF PARTS OF CARCASS OF WHITE PLYMOUTH ROCK COCKERELS WITH INCREASE IN DEVELOPMENT

Approximate slaughter weight	0.5 lb.	1 lb.	1.5 lbs.	2 lbs.	3 lbs.	4 lbs.	5 lbs.	6 lbs.	7 lbs.
Age in days	29	43–57	71	103	117	169	177	250	324
Empty weight	100	196	295	448	604	799	998	1 162	1 473
OFFAL									
Feathers	100	183	344	495	892	1 441	1 871	2 194	1 978
Blood	100	220	319	505	582	791	1 044	1 165	1 648
Head	100	158	225	275	358	450	508	592	850
Shanks and feet	100	209	325	509	745	864	1 027	1 036	1 182
Total offal	100	191	300	437	630	857	1 070	1 196	1 367
VISCERA									
Heart	100	171	218	271	329	429	547	659	1 235
Liver	100	196	246	284	380	456	570	646	532
Kidneys[a]	100	112	132	155	195	215	285	327	310
Pancreas	100	164	195	267	267	336	445	400	491
Spleen	100	225	425	475	675	725	1 000	1 000	875
Lungs	100	200	254	323	515	700	915	869	1 054
Digestive tract	100	200	267	383	433	497	637	667	613
Total viscera	100	201	249	338	400	469	599	648	677
DRESSED CARCASS									
Skin	100	236	350	507	650	907	1 250	1 357	1 943
Neck	100	187	262	475	600	787	912	1 062	1 337
Legs above hock	100	217	346	557	800	1 089	1 363	1 594	2 266
Wings	100	193	286	443	621	807	907	1 064	1 300
Torso	100	207	311	463	663	924	1 170	1 441	1 859
Total dressed carcass	100	210	320	495	693	948	1 188	1 406	1 888
Total bone in dressed carcass	100	185	279	474	626	846	1 031	1 072	1 308
Total flesh and fat in dressed carcass (exclusive of skin)	100	248	389	598	872	1 150	1 474	1 870	2 709
Total flesh, fat, and edible viscera	100	221	336	501	714	922	1 187	1 467	2 041

[a]Assuming a weight of 4.0 grams for the kidneys of the birds weighing 0.5 pound.

The increase in weight of the different parts of the carcass and the different visceral organs relative to the weights in the .5-pound chicks is shown for the cockerels in Table 19. In this table the weights for the different parts of the .5-pound chicks are taken as 100, and the weights in the groups of increasing weight are expressed in percentage of the corresponding weights in the .5-pound group. A study of Table 19 gives much the same information as the study just concluded. Thus,

TABLE 20.—AVERAGE WEIGHTS OF PARTS OF CARCASS OF WHITE PLYMOUTH ROCK PULLETS KILLED AT DIFFERENT WEIGHTS, EXPRESSED IN PERCENTAGE OF THE CORRESPONDING WEIGHTS OF THE COCKERELS

Approximate slaughter weight	2 lbs.	3 lbs.	4 lbs.	5 lbs.
Age in days	73	94	189	219
Empty weight in grams	94	99	104	105
OFFAL	perct.	perct.	perct.	perct.
Feathers	143	130	114	96
Blood	74	77	82	83
Head	85	86	91	87
Shanks and feet	82	74	69	71
Total offal	96	95	92	86
VISCERA				
Heart	98	96	116	109
Liver	105	93	86	96
Kidneys	100	104	114	122
Pancreas	97	100	116	100
Spleen	126	111	114	120
Lungs	100	99	88	75
Gizzard	103	100	109	92
Digestive tract, total	99	100	113	101
Total viscera	94	99	106	100
DRESSED CARCASS				
Skin	103	113	129	128
Neck	92	94	83	84
Legs above hock	86	92	90	90
Wings	92	94	86	96
Torso	103	113	123	127
Total dressed carcass	95	103	106	109
Total bone in dressed carcass	87	92	81	83
Total flesh and fat in dressed carcass	96	105	117	118
Total flesh, fat, and edible viscera	97	104	115	115

while the empty weight of the birds increases at a body weight of 7 pounds to a value 14.73 times the empty weight of .5-pound birds, the total offal increases 13.67 times, the total viscera 6.77 times, and the total dressed carcass 18.88 times. The bones in the carcass increase in weight 13.08 times, while the total flesh and fat increase 27.09 times.

A comparison between the pullets, capons, and cockerels relative to the weights of the different parts of the carcass and the different visceral organs at different body weights, is afforded by the data given in Tables 20 and 21. In these tables the weights of the different parts and organs for each group of pullets and capons are expressed as percentages of the corresponding weights for the cockerels.

TABLE 21.—AVERAGE WEIGHT OF PARTS OF CARCASS OF WHITE PLYMOUTH ROCK CAPONS KILLED AT DIFFERENT WEIGHTS, EXPRESSED IN PERCENTAGE OF THE CORRESPONDING WEIGHTS FOR THE COCKERELS

Approximate slaughter weight	3 lbs.	4 lbs.	5 lbs.	6 lbs.	7 lbs.
Age in days	88	170	180	215	240
Empty weight in grams	101	96	103	103	97
OFFAL	perct.	perct.	perct.	perct.	perct.
Feathers	104	105	102	99	121
Blood	102	93	101	86	75
Head	93	94	93	84	69
Shanks and feet	94	93	98	113	95
Total offal	98	98	100	97	93
VISCERA					
Heart	109	94	98	98	65
Liver	107	100	109	100	167
Kidneys	108	119	106	108	131
Pancreas	93	100	100	127	100
Spleen	104	141	115	147	183
Lungs	101	108	93	113	94
Gizzard	100	104	86	109	120
Digestive tract	101	101	102	116	125
Total viscera	102	101	101	109	113
DRESSED CARCASS					
Skin	109	107	109	120	100
Neck	100	92	95	96	83
Legs above hock	95	91	100	95	77
Wings	99	93	103	99	100
Torso	109	95	105	111	113
Total dressed carcass	102	96	103	105	96
Total bone in dressed carcass	98	97	97	106	97
Total flesh and fat in dressed carcass	103	89	102	101	93
Total flesh, fat, and edible viscera	103	91	101	101	96

The weights of the total offal are consistently less for the pullets than for the cockerels (Table 20). This is true of each division of the offal except the feathers. The weights of feathers for the pullets were generally greater than those for the cockerels, the differences decreasing with advancing body weight. The total weights of viscera did not differ greatly for cockerels and pullets, this being particularly true of the pancreas, liver, and the digestive tract. When the pullets reached a weight of 2 pounds, their lungs weighed the same as the lungs of the cockerels, but with increasing body weight the lungs of the cockerels weighed increasingly more than those of the pullets. Just the reverse is true with the kidneys, which were heavier in the pullets than in the cockerels, the differences increasing with increasing body weight. The weights of spleen were consistently heavier for the pullets than for the cockerels. The dressed carcass in the pullets was always slightly heavier than in the cockerels for body weights of 3 pounds or more, this being entirely referable to the weights of the skin and of torso. For the other parts of the carcass, particularly for the neck, the cockerel weights are consistently greater than the pullet weights. The weights of bone in the dressed carcass were always

TABLE 22.—DIFFERENCES BETWEEN COCKERELS AND CAPONS WEIGHING SEVEN POUNDS IN THE WEIGHTS OF CERTAIN VISCERAL ORGANS
(All weights are in grams)

Kind and No. of bird	Heart	Liver[a]	Spleen	Gizzard	Intestines	Kidneys
COCKERELS						
2115.....	26.0	45	3.4	66	69	13.0
2174.....	20.9	42	4.1	60	75	12.1
2713.....	21.4	48	4.0	70	91	14.8
2825.....	17.3	32	3.0	62	63	11.0
2111.....	19.9	41	3.1	72	59	11.3
CAPONS						
2755.....	13.5	77	8.1	74	101	13.8
2152.....	15.7	66	7.0	78	136	16.8
2614.....	10.9	59	5.0	78	96	18.3
2482.....	12.7	73	7.1	67	94	13.6
2761.....	15.0	74	4.7	98	101	18.5

[a]The weight of gall bladder is included in the weight of liver.

greater at the same body weight for cockerels than for pullets, while the total flesh and fat were always greater for the pullets at body weights of 3 pounds or more.

The differences between cockerels and capons are not so consistent as those between cockerels and pullets. The weights of offal were much the same for capons and cockerels at all ages, except for the weights of head and of blood, which at body weights of more than 5 pounds were greater in the cockerels than in the capons, the difference increasing with increasing body weight. The weights of viscera also were much the same for cockerels and capons for similar body weights, except for the 7-pound weight, at which the total viscera for the capons weighed 13 percent more than for the cockerels.

Some interesting differences between the two groups appear at the 7-pound weight with reference to the heart, liver, spleen, kidney, and digestive tract. While the marked differences in the weights of heart, kidney, and liver were only evident at the 7-pound weight, the differences in the weights of spleen and digestive tract were also evident at smaller weights. For the spleen, in fact, the capons showed consistently greater weights than the cockerels, from body weights of 3 to 7 pounds inclusive. To illustrate the great significance of these differences in the two groups of birds at 7 pounds body weight, Table 22, giving the individual weights for all ten birds, is presented.

Altho considerable variation is evident among the individual birds in each group with respect to the weights of these visceral organs, the differences between cockerels and capons are distinct. For example, in the case of the heart all of the 5 cockerels showed larger weights than any of the 5 capons, while in the case of the liver, spleen, and

TABLE 23.—CHEMICAL COMPOSITION OF THE BONE SAMPLES

Kind of bird and weight	Dry substance	Crude protein (Nx 6.0)	Ash	Ether extract	Unaccounted for	Gross energy per gram
COCKERELS						
lbs.	*perct.*	*perct.*	*perct.*	*perct.*	*perct.*	*small cals.*
0.5..............	39.97	19.68	8.81	4.57	6.91	1 703
1..............	41.46	17.40	11.30	9.86	2.90	1 978
1..............	39.36	18.72	11.23	6.87	2.54	1 572
1.5..............	42.42	19.20	12.52	8.86	1.84	1 810
2..............	44.40	17.76	10.34	14.75	1.55	2 243
3..............	45.00	18.42	11.19	11.70	3.69	2 046
4..............	45.26	19.86	12.56	12.20	0.64	2 194
5..............	47.61	18.54	14.44	13.30	1.33	2 273
6..............	51.37	18.84	16.51	14.47	1.55	2 459
7..............	50.77	20.16	15.73	12.26	2.62	2 317
PULLETS						
lbs.						
2..............	45.40	18.18	11.35	13.57	2.30	2 145
3..............	44.35	18.00	10.07	13.57	2.71	2 185
4..............	51.86	17.76	12.70	18.30	3.10	2 505
5..............	54.87	18.78	14.30	20.00	1.79	2 955
CAPONS						
lbs.						
3..............	44.40	18.30	10.84	13.40	1.86	2 223
4..............	46.75	18.24	11.82	13.54	3.15	2 491
5..............	48.12	18.72	11.57	16.15	1.68	2 628
6..............	50.76	18.84	14.65	15.33	1.94	2 597
7..............	52.95	17.34	11.86	21.62	2.07	2 919

intestines, all the capons showed larger weights than any of the cockerels. For the gizzard and kidney there is a slight overlapping by the two groups, but nevertheless the differences appear to be highly significant. Apparently castration has profoundly affected the growth of these visceral organs, either directly or indirectly.

These differences in organ weights between capons and cockerels, so far as they relate to the heart, spleen, and kidneys, are in agreement with results reported by Marrassini and Luciani.[7] These authors explain the hypertrophy of the spleen in castrated birds as a consequence of the peritoneal hemorrhages often resulting from the removal of the testicles in fowls. This explanation is hardly consistent, however, with the progressive divergence in spleen weights among cockerels and capons of increasing weight. The difference in heart weight between castrated and uncastrated male birds may be reasonably explained as the result of a greater muscular activity of the cockerels. Hatai[8] has shown that among groups of rats receiving different

TABLE 24.—CHEMICAL COMPOSITION OF THE SAMPLES OF FLESH AND EDIBLE VISCERA

Kind of bird and weight	Dry substance	Crude protein (N x 6.0)	Crude fat	Ash	Unaccounted for	Gross energy per gram
COCKERELS						
lbs.	perct.	perct.	perct.	perct.	perct.	small cals.
0.5.........	30.07	20.88	4.38	1.44	3.37	1 526
1..........	25.40	19.56	3.95	1.27	0.62	1 461
1..........	24.87	19.62	3.55	1.31	0.39	1 281
1.5.........	28.63	20.04	6.54	1.27	0.78	1 540
2..........	27.20	18.84	6.16	1.07	1.13	1 597
3..........	28.51	20.10	4.39	1.13	2.89	1 571
4..........	29.49	21.00	3.92	1.02	3.55	1 460
5..........	28.49	19.74	5.54	1.29	1.92	1 651[a]
6..........	28.51	20.22	5.40	1.72	1.17	1 714
7..........	28.08	21.00	4.46	1.40	1.22	1 606
PULLETS						
lbs.						
2..........	26.70	19.02	6.00	1.06	0.62	1 515
3..........	34.09	18.90	9.75	1.20	4.24	1 860
4..........	30.79	18.54	11.22	1.01	0.02	2 262
5..........	33.67	20.22	12.62	1.35	−0.52	2 356
CAPONS						
lbs.						
3..........	28.20	19.74	5.99	1.27	1.20	1 628
4..........	29.25	19.26	7.16	1.11	1.72	1 787
5..........	33.10	19.38	8.61	1.17	3.94	1 893
6..........	31.43	18.84	10.29	0.98	1.32	2 049
7..........	36.97	18.00	16.84	0.94	1.19	2 543

[a]Calculated by using factors 5.7 calories per gram of protein and 9.5 calories per gram of fat.

amounts of exercise, the weights of the heart observed were positively correlated with the exercise records, while Hoskins[9] and Richter[10] have shown, with the same species of animal, that castration markedly lowers spontaneous activity.

No clear differences exist between cockerels and capons with reference to the dressed carcass and its dissected parts, except possibly with respect to the neck and the legs above hock, the weights of which were, in general, less for the capons than for the cockerels, especially at the 7-pound weight. Also, no consistent differences can be made out between cockerels and capons in the weights of total bone or of total flesh and fat in the dressed carcass.

CHEMICAL COMPOSITION OF THE BIRDS AT DIFFERENT WEIGHTS

Each group of 5 birds was analyzed in three composite samples: first, the total bone of the dressed carcass; second, the flesh and fat of the dressed carcass plus the heart, liver, and gizzard; and third, the offal sample, including the blood, feathers, head, shanks and feet, gall

TABLE 25.—CHEMICAL COMPOSITION OF THE SAMPLES OF OFFAL

Kind of bird and weight	Dry substance	Crude protein (N x 6.0)	Ash	Ether extract	Unaccounted for	Gross energy per gram
COCKERELS						
lbs.	perct.	perct.	perct.	perct.	perct.	small cals.
0.5.........	34.30	22.25	2.56	6.63	2.86	1 762
1..........	29.74	21.12	2.36	7.67	−1.41	1 825
1..........	29.73	20.20	2.42	5.33	1.78	1 601
1.5.........	33.86	21.68	2.37	9.36	0.45	1 976
2..........	36.21	21.04	2.39	9.88	2.90	2 092
3..........	37.64	24.72	2.31	9.72	0.89	2 332[b]
4..........	36.78	24.15	1.98	8.77	1.88	2 289
5..........	41.54	25.62	2.01	11.13	2.78	2 137
6..........	53.34	34.02	4.13	13.12	2.07	2 774
7..........	51.69	26.70	2.65	19.89	2.45	3 255
PULLETS						
lbs.						
2..........	40.08	24.16	2.49	11.86	1.57	2 094
3..........	37.86[a]	24.22[a]	2.59[a]	10.35[a]	0.70	2 364[b]
4..........	49.94	25.83	1.89	19.14	3.08	2 758
5..........	51.86	27.71	1.82	23.07	−0.74	3 516
CAPONS						
lbs.						
3..........	38.08	23.72	2.60	10.98	0.78	2 280
4..........	40.65	24.12	2.02	12.12	2.39	2 736
5..........	42.18	22.29	1.85	14.86	3.18	2 803
6..........	54.18	29.45	2.34	18.99	3.40	3 120
7..........	51.37	25.85	2.22	20.87	2.43	3 396

[a]Chemical composition calculated from average composition of offal from 3-pound capons and cockerels.
[b]Calculated by using factors 5.7 calories per gram of protein and 9.5 calories per gram of fat.

bladder, and the viscera not included in the second sample. These samples were all ground in a fresh condition and submitted to routine analysis. The percentage of dry substance in each sample was corrected so far as possible for moisture losses during dissection, weighing, and grinding of the material. The gross energy of each sample was also directly determined in the bomb calorimeter. The results of these analyses and energy determinations are included in Tables 23, 24, and 25. Altho the percentage composition of these samples shows a good deal of irregularity in comparing birds of different weight, there is a fairly general tendency for the dry substance to increase at the heavier weights, and for the ether extract to increase in the samples for the pullets and capons. No consistent increase in the ether extract of the cockerel samples was manifested after a weight of 2

TABLE 26.—PERCENTAGE COMPOSITION OF LIVE BIRDS

Kind of bird and weight	Age at slaughter	Dry substance	Crude protein (N x 6.0)	Crude fat	Ash	Unaccounted for	Gross energy per gram
	days	perct.	perct.	perct.	perct.	perct.	small cals.
CHICKS gms.							
37.5..........	1.5	24.89	16.18	5.60	1.83	1.28	1 476
COCKERELS lbs.							
0.5...........	29	27.84	17.46	4.40	2.82	3.16	1 366
1.............	43	26.96	17.81	5.88	3.13	0.14	1 499
1.............	57	26.57	17.92	4.42	3.23	1.00	1 327
1.5...........	71	30.13	18.65	7.34	3.37	0.77	1 605
2.............	103	31.50	17.97	8.60	3.18	1.75	1 775
3.............	117	32.41	19.86	7.18	3.24	2.13	1 470[a]
4.............	169	32.77	20.35	6.83	3.41	2.18	1 775
5.............	177	34.88	20.46	8.53	3.84	2.05	1 838
6.............	250	38.83	23.41	9.14	4.82	1.46	2 094
7.............	324	37.73	21.58	10.44	3.97	1.74	2 235
PULLETS lbs.							
2.............	73	31.89	18.82	8.82	3.19	1.06	1 676
3.............	94	34.92	19.37	9.97	3.08	2.50	1 967
4.............	189	38.58	19.81	14.29	2.95	1.53	2 329
5.............	219	40.19	20.99	16.19	3.24	−0.23	2 650
CAPONS lbs.							
3.............	88	32.21	19.35	8.51	3.27	1.08	1 833
4.............	170	34.99	19.74	9.74	3.37	2.14	2 156
5.............	180	37.10	19.16	11.68	3.22	3.04	2 236
6.............	215	40.30	21.22	13.41	3.62	2.05	2 370
7.............	240	41.62	19.23	17.78	2.95	1.66	2 707

[a]The estimated energy value of this group, using average factors for protein and fat, is 1,814 small calories per gram.

pounds was reached. The energy value per gram of the different samples varied closely in accordance with their content of ether extract.

From the relative weights of the different samples for each group of birds and their chemical composition, the composition of the live birds was calculated. The values thus obtained are given in Table 26. For comparison, the average composition of 5 White Plymouth Rock chicks shortly after hatching is given. These data on baby chicks were obtained in connection with another experiment. The percentage of dry substance increased very regularly with advancing age and size, attaining higher figures for the pullets and capons than for the cockerels. On the other hand, the percentages of ash and protein were generally larger for the cockerels than for the pullets or capons for any given weight. Pullets show a much more marked ten-

TABLE 27.—PERCENTAGE COMPOSITION OF BIRDS ON BASIS OF EMPTY WEIGHT

Kind of bird and weight	Dry substance	Crude protein (N x 6.0)	Crude fat	Ash	Gross energy per gram
COCKERELS					
lbs.	perct.	perct.	perct.	perct.	small cals.
0.5.........	29.94	18.77	4.75	3.00	1 474
1...........	28.92	19.10	6.30	3.35	1 598
1...........	28.19	18.86	4.65	3.40	1 404
1.5........	31.83	19.70	7.75	3.56	1 695
2...........	32.36	18.47	8.83	3.26	1 819
3...........	33.80	20.71	7.49	3.38	1 533[a]
4...........	33.92	21.07	7.07	3.53	1 838
5.:.........	36.17	21.22	8.90	3.98	1 908
6...........	39.97	24.09	9.41	4.96	2 149
7...........	38.61	22.08	10.67	4.06	2 213
PULLETS					
lbs.					
2...........	33.62	19.85	9.19	3.35	1 766
3...........	36.24	20.10	10.35	3.19	2 042
4...........	39.76	20.42	13.61	3.04	2 401
5...........	41.90	21.88	16.88	3.38	2 762
CAPONS					
lbs.					
3...........	33.68	20.23	8.90	3.42	1 916
4...........	35.98	20.30	10.02	3.47	2 217
5...........	38.11	19.68	12.00	3.30	2 297
6...........	41.76	21.99	13.90	3.75	2 456
7...........	42.90	19.82	18.33	3.06	2 790

[a]The estimated energy value of this group, using average factors for protein and fat, is 1,872 small calories per gram.

dency to fatten than cockerels, the capons occupying an intermediate position in this respect (Table 26). The energy value per gram of the pullets for weights of 3 pounds or above were also distinctly higher than the energy values for either cockerels or capons.

The close agreement between the composition of the two groups of 1-pound cockerels killed two weeks apart is noteworthy, indicating that the chemical as well as the anatomical composition of the birds is more a function of the growth attained than of the age. In further support of this statement, the distinct difference in chemical composition between the 1-pound and 1.5-pound cockerels slaughtered two weeks apart may be pointed out.

For some purposes it is preferable to express the chemical composition of animals on the basis of the empty weights. This has been done in Table 27 for the birds slaughtered in this experiment. The differences between the values in Table 27 and those in Table 26, however, are so small that they call for no further discussion.

TABLE 28.—PERCENTAGE DISTRIBUTION OF DRY MATTER AND PROTEIN AMONG (1) EDIBLE FLESH AND VISCERA, (2) BONES OF THE DRESSED CARCASS, AND (3) OFFAL IN BIRDS OF DIFFERENT WEIGHTS AND SEX

Kind of bird and weight	Dry matter			Protein		
	Edible flesh, etc.	Bones of dressed carcass	Offal	Edible flesh, etc.	Bones of dressed carcass	Offal
COCKERELS						
lbs.	perct.	perct.	perct.	perct.	perct.	perct.
0.5.........	33.6	23.7	42.7	37.2	18.6	44.2
1..........	35.0	24.1	40.9	41.1	16.3	42.6
1.5........	36.5	22.8	40.7	41.2	16.7	42.1
2..........	33.2	26.1	40.7	40.2	18.3	41.4
3..........	35.6	24.8	39.6	41.0	16.5	42.5
4..........	36.1	25.5	38.3	41.5	18.0	40.5
5..........	33.6	24.6	41.8	39.7	16.3	44.0
6..........	32.3	21.4	46.3	38.0	13.0	49.0
7..........	34.7	21.1	44.2	45.3	14.6	40.0
PULLETS						
lbs.						
2..........	32.9	23.9	43.2	39.7	16.2	44.1
3..........	41.6	21.1	37.2	41.6	15.5	42.9
4..........	35.9	19.5	44.5	42.1	13.0	44.8
5..........	37.7	19.3	42.9	43.4	12.7	43.9
CAPONS						
lbs.						
3..........	36.0	23.8	40.2	42.0	16.3	41.7
4..........	33.1	25.0	41.9	38.6	17.3	44.1
5..........	36.2	23.4	40.4	41.1	17.6	41.3
6..........	33.4	20.6	45.9	38.0	14.6	47.4
7..........	41.3	19.6	39.1	43.5	13.9	42.6

The distribution of dry matter, protein, ether extract, energy, and mineral matter among the three composite samples is expressed in percentages in Tables 28, 29, and 30. The offal sample contained a large proportion, namely from 40 to 50 percent (average 41.7 percent), of the dry substance in the birds at all weights. Furthermore, there is no clear distinction between the different groups of birds in this respect, nor can any progressive change in the percentage be noted with increasing size and age. The edible part of the carcass contains an average of 35.5 percent of the total dry matter, 40.8 percent of the total protein, 30.2 percent of the total ether extract, and 37.2 percent of the total gross energy of the birds at all weights. For the pullets, the percentage of the total fat and energy contained in the edible flesh and viscera seemed to be distinctly larger for weights of 3 pounds and over, than the similar percentages for the cockerels and capons. The mineral matter in the carcasses was contained largely in the bone sample, which contained an average of 61.1 percent. The offal sample ranked next with an average of 24.2 percent, and the edible flesh

TABLE 29.—PERCENTAGE DISTRIBUTION OF ETHER EXTRACT AND GROSS ENERGY AMONG (1) EDIBLE FLESH AND VISCERA, (2) BONES OF THE DRESSED CARCASS, AND (3) OFFAL IN BIRDS OF DIFFERENT WEIGHTS AND SEX

Kind of bird and weight	Ether extract			Gross energy		
	Edible flesh, etc.	Bones of dressed carcass	Offal	Edible flesh, etc.	Bones of dressed carcass	Offal
COCKERELS lbs.	perct.	perct.	perct.	perct.	perct.	perct.
0.5.........	30.9	17.1	52.0	34.6	20.8	44.7
1..........	27.3	26.1	46.7	35.0	20.2	44.8
1.5........	34.2	19.5	46.3	36.9	18.3	44.8
2..........	27.5	31.8	40.7	34.7	23.4	41.9
3..........	24.8	29.0	46.2	43.2	24.8	32.0
4..........	23.1	33.1	43.9	33.1	22.8	44.1
5..........	26.6	27.9	45.6	37.0	22.2	40.8
6..........	26.0	25.6	48.4	36.1	19.1	44.8
7..........	19.9	18.4	61.6	34.6	16.8	48.6
PULLETS lbs.						
2..........	27.1	26.2	46.7	35.5	21.5	43.0
3..........	41.7	22.7	35.6	40.3	18.5	41.2
4..........	35.3	18.6	46.1	43.7	15.6	40.7
5..........	35.1	17.5	47.4	40.0	15.8	44.2
CAPONS lbs.						
3..........	29.0	27.2	43.8	36.6	21.0	42.4
4..........	29.2	26.1	44.9	32.7	21.6	45.7
5..........	29.9	24.9	45.1	34.4	21.2	44.4
6..........	32.8	18.7	48.4	37.0	18.0	45.0
7..........	44.0	18.8	37.2	43.7	16.6	39.7

sample contained only 14.7 percent. In general, the percentage of the mineral matter of the carcass contained in the bones of the dressed carcass tended to increase with increasing size and age, while the percentage contained in the offal tended to decrease.

From the chemical composition of the flesh and fat of the dressed carcass and of the edible viscera (exclusive of heart and kidneys), and from the weights of this fraction of the carcass (corrected to even body weights), the total edible nutrients in White Plymouth Rock chickens of different live weights may be calculated. The results of such a calculation are given in Table 31. The outstanding feature of this tabulation is the demonstration of the superiority of pullets in their content of edible fat and energy, unaccompanied by any inferiority in the content of edible protein. Capons rank next to pullets in regard to the content of edible fat and energy, but are inferior to cockerels in the content of edible protein.

Altho the different groups of birds were killed at average weights approximating closely the weights given in the left column of the tables just considered, it was only an approximation. In computing

TABLE 30.—PERCENTAGE DISTRIBUTION OF MINERAL MATTER AMONG (1) EDIBLE FLESH AND VISCERA, (2) BONES OF THE DRESSED CARCASS, AND (3) OFFAL IN BIRDS OF DIFFERENT WEIGHTS AND SEX

Kind of bird and weight	Crude ash		
	Edible flesh, etc.	Bones of dressed carcass	Offal
COCKERELS			
lbs.	perct.	perct.	perct.
0.5	16.1	52.2	31.7
1	15.2	57.1	27.7
1.5	14.4	60.1	25.5
2	13.0	60.4	26.7
3	14.1	61.6	24.3
4	12.0	68.1	19.8
5	13.9	67.8	18.4
6	15.7	55.4	28.9
7	16.4	62.0	21.6
PULLETS			
lbs.			
2	13.0	60.1	26.9
3	16.6	54.5	28.9
4	15.4	62.6	22.1
5	18.8	62.5	18.7
CAPONS			
lbs.			
3	16.0	57.1	26.9
4	13.0	65.5	21.5
5	14.8	64.8	20.4
6	11.6	66.3	22.1
7	14.7	61.6	23.7

the composition of gains within any weight interval of the cockerels, pullets, and capons, it is necessary to compute the composition of birds at the exact weights under consideration. This is done in Table 32 by applying the percentages contained in Table 26 to the even weights of .5, 1, 1.5, and 2 pounds, etc. The total energy content per bird has been estimated (at each weight) from the content of the crude protein and crude fat (Table 32, last column). In this estimation the energy values of protein and fat have been taken as 5.7 and 9.5 calories per gram, respectively. These factors have been used by Armsby for similar computations on the larger farm animals. A comparison of this column of figures with the gross energy content as directly determined gives some idea concerning the size of error that would be made in applying these average factors to the protein and fat of chicken carcasses. As a general rule, the estimated energy content is higher than the content as directly determined, the average difference amounting to 3.6 percent.

TABLE 31.—EDIBLE NUTRIENTS IN WHITE PLYMOUTH ROCK BIRDS OF DIFFERENT WEIGHTS AND SEX

Kind of bird and weight	Weight of flesh and edible viscera	Dry matter	Crude protein	Crude fat	Ash	Gross energy
COCKERELS						
lbs.	gms.	gms.	gms.	gms.	gms.	cals.
0.5.........	64	19.4	13.4	2.8	0.9	98
1..........	166	42.1	32.4	6.5	2.1	242
1..........	177	43.9	34.6	6.3	2.3	226
1.5........	254	72.6	50.8	16.6	3.2	391
2..........	348	94.8	65.6	21.5	3.7	556
3..........	551	157	111	24.2	6.2	866
4..........	729	215	153	28.6	7.4	1 064
5..........	934	266	184	51.7	12.0	1 542
6..........	1 198	342	242	64.7	20.6	2 053
7..........	1 480	416	311	66.0	20.7	2 376
PULLETS						
lbs.						
2..........	356	95.2	67.8	21.4	3.8	540
3..........	580	198	110	56.6	6.1	1 079
4..........	811	250	150	91.0	8.2	1 834
5..........	1 022	344	207	129	13.8	2 408
CAPONS						
lbs.						
3..........	561	158	111	33.6	7.1	913
4..........	718	210	138	51.4	8.0	1 283
5..........	922	305	179	79.4	10.8	1 745
6..........	1 166	366	220	120	11.4	2 389
7..........	1 477	546	266	249	13.9	3 755

The data in Table 32 must form the basis for the estimation of the composition of successive gains in weight of the birds from .5 to 7 pounds. They are too irregular, however, to permit of accurate estimates, mainly because of the small size of the groups of birds analyzed at each weight. Under these circumstances it is to be expected that the error in computing the composition of successive small gains in weight from such data would be considerable. For example, the error in assuming that the 5 cockerels killed and analyzed at a weight of 5 pounds possessed the same composition at a weight of 4 pounds as the 5 other cockerels killed at that weight, will be contained in full in the estimate of the composition of the gain from 4 to 5 pounds. This error, inherent in slaughter experiments of this type, may be decreased only by increasing the number of birds killed at each weight or by smoothing off the data obtained on the smaller groups of birds by the proper mathematical procedure. The latter expedient was adopted, and it was found that the relation between the content of the birds in dry matter, protein, etc., and the live weight of the bird,

TABLE 32.—CALCULATED COMPOSITION OF THE BIRDS AT EVEN WEIGHTS

Kind of bird and weight	Dry substance	Crude protein (Nx 6.0)	Crude fat	Ash	Unaccounted for	Gross energy	Estimated gross energy[a]
COCKERELS							
lbs.	*gms.*	*gms.*	*gms.*	*gms.*	*gms.*	*therms*	*therms*
0.5............	63	40	10	6	7	0.31	0.32
1.............	121	81	23	14	3	0.64	0.68
1.5............	205	127	50	23	5	1.09	1.20
2.............	286	163	78	29	16	1.61	1.67
3.............	441	270	98	44	29	2.00	2.47
4.............	594	369	124	62	39	3.22	3.28
5.............	791	464	195	86	46	4.32	4.50
6.............	1 057	637	249	131	40	5.70	6.00
7.............	1 198	685	331	126	56	7.10	7.05
PULLETS							
lbs.							
2.............	289	171	80	29	9	1.52	1.73
3.............	475	264	136	42	33	2.68	2.80
4.............	700	359	259	54	28	4.22	4.51
5.............	912	476	367	74	−5	6.01	6.20
CAPONS							
lbs.							
3.............	438	263	116	45	14	2.49	2.60
4.............	635	358	177	61	39	3.91	3.72
5.............	842	435	265	73	69	5.07	5.00
6.............	1 097	578	365	99	55	6.45	6.76
7.............	1 322	611	565	94	52	8.59	8.85

[a]These values were estimated by using factors 5.7 calories per gram for protein and 9.5 calories per gram for fat.

can be very well represented for the range of live weight included in this experiment by a parabolic equation of the type $y = ax + bx^2$.

This equation has been fitted to each of the relations between the different chemical constituents and live weight for each of the three groups of birds. In dealing with the results for pullets and capons, it has been assumed that pullets weighing less than 2 pounds would have the same composition as cockerels of equal weight, and that the composition of capons before castration is well represented by the composition of the cockerels slaughtered between .5 and 2 pounds inclusive. The equation has been fitted to each set of experimental data by the method of least squares. A graphical picture of the closeness of fit of the mathematical curves to the experimental data is given in Figs. 1 to 5 inclusive.[a]

An inspection of these charts seems to indicate that the closeness of fit of the curves to the experimental data is satisfactory. The fact that the relation between the content of these birds in any given nutrient, and the slaughter weight, is such that it can well be represented by a mathematical equation of this simple type, again testifies to the

TABLE 33.—COMPOSITION OF THE BIRDS AT EVEN WEIGHTS AS COMPUTED FROM MATHEMATICAL EQUATIONS FITTED TO THE DATA IN TABLE 31

Kind of bird and weight	Dry substance	Crude protein	Crude fat	Ash	Unaccounted for	Gross energy
COCKERELS						
lbs.	*gms.*	*gms.*	*gms.*	*gms.*	*gms.*	*cals.*
0.5.........	64.2	41.2	12.4	6.7	3.9	290
1.........	131.7	83.5	26.4	13.7	8.1	615
1.5.........	202.4	127.1	42.0	21.1	12.2	971
2.........	276.5	171.9	59.2	28.9	16.5	1 361
3.........	434.8	265.1	98.5	45.5	25.3	2 239
4.........	605.4	363.1	144.4	63.6	34.3	3 249
5.........	789.4	465.9	196.6	83.1	43.8	4 390
6.........	986.6	573.6	255.4	104.0	53.6	5 663
7.........	1 196.9	686.1	320.7	126.4	63.7	7 067
8.........	1 420.3	803.4	392.4	150.5	74.0	8 603
PULLETS						
lbs.						
0.5.........	62.6	39.8	9.6	6.8	6.4	276
1.........	131.8	81.2	25.4	13.8	11.4	624
1.5.........	207.5	124.3	47.2	20.8	15.2	1 043
2.........	289.8	169.1	75.1	27.9	17.7	1 534
3.........	474.1	263.7	149.2	42.4	18.8	2 732
4.........	684.6	365.0	247.7	57.1	14.8	4 218
5.........	921.4	472.9	370.5	72.2	5.8	5 990
6.........	1 184.5	587.5	517.7	87.6	−8.3	8 050
CAPONS						
lbs.						
0.5.........	61.1	43.0	6.4	8.0	3.7	313
1.........	127.5	86.0	17.7	15.8	8.0	671
1.5.........	199.1	129.3	33.8	23.4	12.6	1 073
2.........	275.9	172.6	54.7	30.9	17.7	1 520
3.........	445.4	259.8	111.0	45.2	29.4	2 546
4.........	635.9	347.4	186.7	58.8	43.0	3 750
5.........	847.3	435.6	281.7	71.6	58.4	5 132
6.........	1 079.8	524.4	396.1	83.7	75.6	6 692
7.........	1 333.3	613.7	529.8	95.1	94.7	8 430
8.........	1 607.8	703.5	682.9	105.7	115.7	10 346

[a]In determining the constants of the equations, no account was taken of the experimental data for the 6-pound cockerels relating to dry matter, crude protein, and ash, or of the data for the 6-pound capons relating to protein and ash. These results appear to be so far out of line with the others as to justify their exclusion.

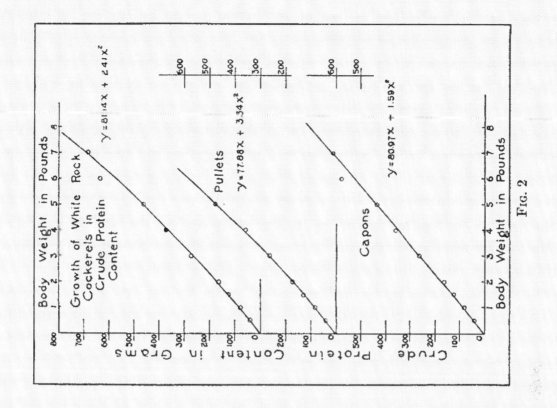

FIG. 2

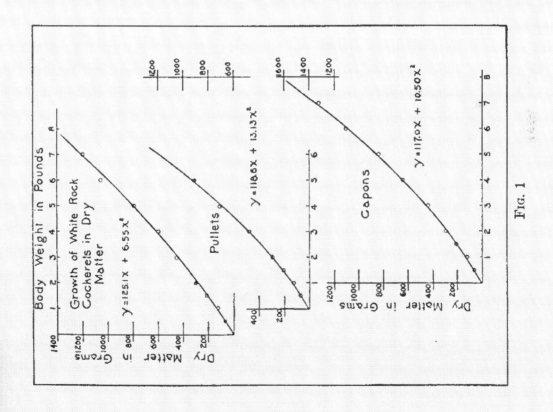

FIG. 1

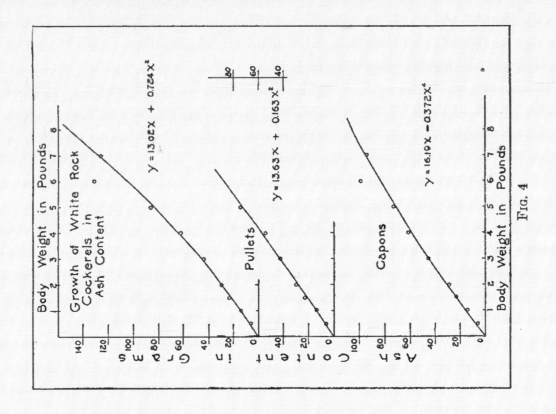

Growth of White Rock Cockerels in Ash Content

$y = 13.02X + 0.724X^2$

Pullets

$y = 13.63X + 0.163X^2$

Capons

$y = 16.19X - 0.372X^2$

Body Weight in Pounds

Fig. 4

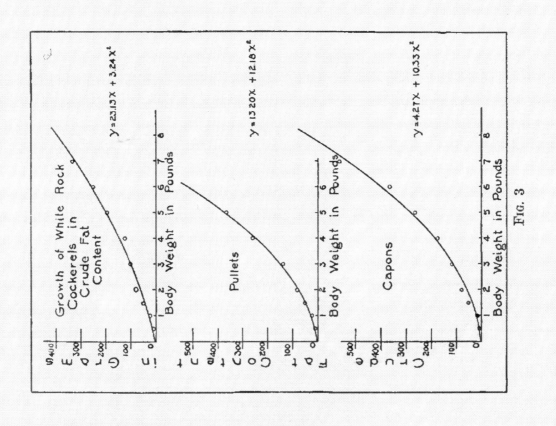

Growth of White Rock Cockerels in Crude Fat Content

$y = 23.13X + 3.24X^2$

Pullets

$y = 13.20X + 12.18X^2$

Capons

$y = 4.27X + 10.33X^2$

Body Weight in Pounds

Fig. 3

conclusion that the composition of birds is more closely related to the growth attained than to the age.

By means of the mathematical equations fitting the various sets of experimental results contained in Table 32, it is possible to estimate the composition of birds at even weights, obtaining in this way a smoothed set of data from which the composition of successive gains may be computed with greater accuracy than from the unsmoothed experimental data themselves. This has been done in Table 33. The

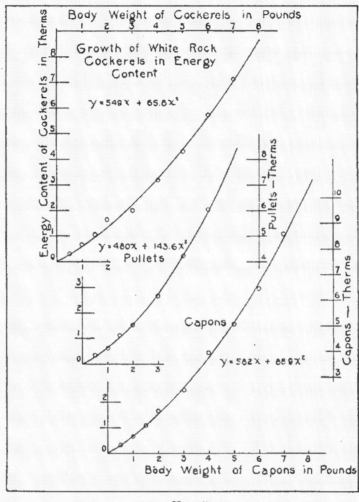

Fig. 5

composition of the three groups of birds at weights 1 pound heavier than the greatest actual slaughter weight has been estimated by the mathematical equations. Any more extensive extrapolation, however, would not be advisable. Corrected estimates of the percentage composition of the birds at successive even weights may be computed from the data in Table 33. This has been done in Table 34. Table 35 contains the estimates of the composition of the successive pound gains in weight of cockerels, pullets, and capons based upon the smoothed data contained in Table 33. The content of the successive pound gains in dry matter, protein, fat, ash, and energy increases in a linear fashion with the live weight of the birds, a result which follows from the fact that the relation between the content of the birds in each of these constituents and the live weight may be represented by a parabolic equation.[a]

It is evident that the energy value of the gains put on by pullets exceeds the energy value of gains for the other two groups of birds, while the capon gains rank next in this respect. For example, the gain from 4 to 5 pounds on the pullets contained a decidedly greater gross energy content than the 7- to 8-pound gain on the cockerels, and was

TABLE 34.—PERCENTAGE COMPOSITION OF THE BIRDS AT EVEN WEIGHTS COMPUTED FROM TABLE 33

Kind of bird and weight	Dry substance	Crude protein	Crude fat	Ash	Unaccounted for	Gross energy per gram
COCKERELS						
lbs.	perct.	perct.	perct.	perct.	perct.	small cals.
0.5	28.31	18.17	5.47	2.95	1.72	1 279
1	29.03	18.41	5.82	3.02	1.78	1 356
1.5	29.75	18.68	6.17	3.10	1.80	1 427
2	30.48	18.95	6.53	3.19	1.81	1 500
3	31.92	19.48	7.24	3.34	1.86	1 645
4	33.37	20.01	7.96	3.51	1.89	1 791
5	34.81	20.54	8.67	3.66	1.94	1 936
6	36.25	21.08	9.38	3.82	1.97	2 081
7	37.70	21.61	10.10	3.98	2.01	2 226
8	39.14	22.14	10.81	4.15	2.04	2 371
PULLETS						
lbs.						
0.5	27.60	17.55	4.23	3.00	2.82	1 217
1	29.06	17.90	5.60	3.04	2.52	1 376
1.5	30.50	18.27	6.94	3.06	2.23	1 533
2	31.94	18.64	8.28	3.08	1.94	1 691
3	34.84	19.38	10.96	3.12	1.38	2 008
4	37.73	20.12	13.65	3.15	0.81	2 325
5	40.63	20.85	16.34	3.18	0.26	2 641
6	43.52	21.59	19.02	3.22	−0.31	2 958
CAPONS						
lbs						
0.5	26.94	18.96	2.82	3.53	1.63	1 380
1	28.11	18.96	3.90	3.48	1.77	1 479
1.5	29.26	19.00	4.97	3.44	1.85	1 577
2	30.41	19.03	6.03	3.41	1.94	1 675
3	32.73	19.09	8.16	3.32	2.16	1 871
4	35.05	19.15	10.30	3.24	2.36	2 067
5	37.36	19.21	12.42	3.16	2.57	2 263
6	39.68	19.27	14.55	3.08	2.78	2 459
7	41.99	19.33	16.69	3.00	2.97	2 655
8	44.31	19.39	18.82	2.91	3.19	2 851

[a] See Lipka, J., "Graphical and Mechanical Computation," p. 146. John Wiley and Sons, 1918.

slightly greater than the 6- to 7-pound gain on the capons. This relation of the energy content of gains is directly related to their content in crude fat. Evidently pullets fatten at a much more rapid rate than either cockerels or capons. As an illustration of this fact, the 5- to 6-pound gain on the pullets contained over twice as much fat as the 7- to 8-pound gain on the cockerels. At the same time, the pullet gains contained larger amounts of protein than the

TABLE 35.—COMPOSITION OF SUCCESSIVE POUND GAINS IN WEIGHT COMPUTED FROM TABLE 33

Kind of bird	Gain from	Dry substance	Crude protein	Crude fat	Ash	Unaccounted for	Gross energy
	lbs.	gms.	gms.	gms.	gms.	gms.	cals.
COCKERELS.....	0 to 1	131.7	83.5	26.4	13.7	8.1	615
	1 to 2	144.8	88.4	32.8	15.2	8.4	746
	2 to 3	158.1	93.2	39.3	16.6	9.0	878
	3 to 4	171.0	98.0	45.9	18.1	9.0	1 010
	4 to 5	184.0	102.8	52.2	19.5	9.5	1 141
	5 to 6	197.2	107.7	58.8	20.9	9.8	1 273
	6 to 7	210.3	112.5	65.3	22.4	10.1	1 404
	7 to 8	223.4	117.3	71.7	24.1	10.3	1 536
PULLETS.......	0 to 1	131.8	81.2	25.4	13.8	11.4	624
	1 to 2	158.0	87.9	49.7	14.1	6.3	910
	2 to 3	184.3	94.6	74.1	14.5	1.1	1 198
	3 to 4	210.5	101.3	98.5	14.7	−4.0	1 486
	4 to 5	236.8	107.9	122.8	15.1	−9.0	1 772
	5 to 6	263.1	114.6	147.2	15.4	−14.1	2 060
CAPONS........	0 to 1	127.5	86.0	17.7	15.8	8.0	671
	1 to 2	148.4	86.6	37.0	15.1	9.7	849
	2 to 3	169.5	87.2	56.3	14.3	11.7	1 026
	3 to 4	190.5	87.6	75.7	13.6	13.6	1 204
	4 to 5	211.4	88.2	95.0	12.8	15.4	1 382
	5 to 6	232.5	88.8	114.4	12.1	17.2	1 560
	6 to 7	253.5	89.3	133.7	11.4	19.1	1 738
	7 to 8	274.5	89.8	153.1	10.6	21.0	1 916

cockerel gains, the capon gains ranking last in this respect. This is probably related to the fact that the growth of the pullets represented more of an increase in muscular tissue and less of an increase in bone than the growth of the cockerels.

It is interesting to note that the protein content of the capon gains was very nearly constant thruout the range of growth covered in this experiment. On the other hand, the cockerels outranked all other birds in the ash content of their gains, which increased markedly, while the ash content of the pullet gains was very nearly constant. The computed ash content of the capon gains decreased from beginning to end, but the authors do not attach any great significance to this apparent decrease, because it was evidently dependent upon whether or not the erratic result on the 6-pound capons was considered in determining the constants in the parabolic equation relating to the crude ash content of the birds. The dry matter content of the pullet gains exceeded slightly the dry matter content of the capon gains at equal weight intervals, and greatly exceeded the dry matter content of the cockerel gains.

The results compiled in Table 35 are expressed on a percentage basis in Table 36. These figures reveal the same relationships that

TABLE 36.—PERCENTAGE COMPOSITION OF SUCCESSIVE POUND GAINS IN WEIGHT COMPUTED FROM TABLE 35

Kind of bird	Gain from	Dry substance	Crude protein	Crude fat	Ash	Unaccounted for	Gross energy per gram
	lbs.	perct.	perct.	perct.	perct.	perct.	small cals.
COCKERELS.....	0 to 1	29.03	18.41	5.82	3.02	1.78	1 356
	1 to 2	31.92	19.49	7.23	3.35	1.85	1 645
	2 to 3	34.85	20.55	8.66	3.66	1.98	1 936
	3 to 4	37.70	21.60	10.11	3.99	2.00	2 227
	4 to 5	40.57	22.66	11.50	4.30	2.11	2 515
	5 to 6	43.47	23.74	12.96	4.61	2.16	2 806
	6 to 7	46.36	24.80	14.40	4.94	2.22	3 095
	7 to 8	49.25	25.86	15.81	5.31	2.27	3 386
PULLETS.......	0 to 1	29.06	17.90	5.60	3.04	2.52	1 376
	1 to 2	34.83	19.38	10.96	3.11	1.38	2 006
	2 to 3	40.63	20.86	16.34	3.20	0.23	2 641
	3 to 4	46.41	22.33	21.72	3.24	−0.88	3 276
	4 to 5	52.20	23.79	27.07	3.33	−1.99	3 907
	5 to 6	58.00	25.26	32.45	3.40	−3.11	4 541
CAPONS........	0 to 1	28.11	18.96	3.90	3.48	1.77	1 479
	1 to 2	32.72	19.09	8.16	3.33	2.14	1 872
	2 to 3	37.37	19.22	12.41	3.15	2.59	2 262
	3 to 4	42.00	19.31	16.69	3.00	3.00	2 654
	4 to 5	46.61	19.44	20.94	2.82	3.41	3 047
	5 to 6	51.26	19.58	25.22	2.67	3.79	3 439
	6 to 7	55.89	19.69	29.48	2.51	4.21	3 832
	7 to 8	60.52	19.80	33.75	2.34	4.63	4 224

have already been pointed out. The change in percentage composition of gains with increasing body weight is illustrated graphically in Figs. 6 and 7.

RATE OF RETENTION OF NUTRIENTS DURING GROWTH

The practical value of estimates of the composition of gains in weight of growing animals depends upon the possibility of determining from such data the requirements of growing animals for nutriment. It seems obvious that the amount of energy added to the body of a growing animal daily at different ages is a fair estimate of the amount of net food energy required, above that used for maintenance,

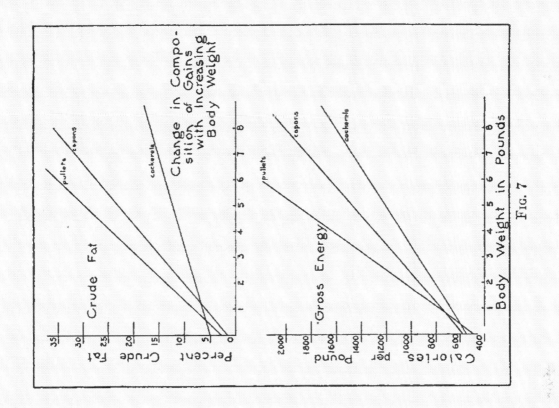

Crude Fat

Change in Composition of Gains with Increasing Body Weight

Gross Energy

Body Weight in Pounds

FIG. 7

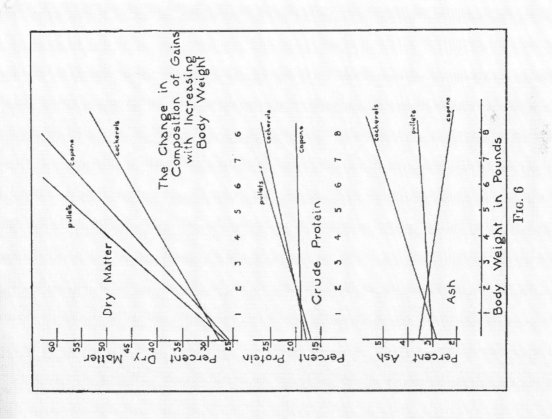

Dry Matter

The Change in Composition of Gains with Increasing Body Weight

Crude Protein

Ash

Body Weight in Pounds

FIG. 6

to sustain normal growth. Such values have been used in this way by Armsby in computing his feeding standards for growth and fattening. Obviously they are of practical significance only when the net energy value of ordinary farm feeds in covering growth requirements is known. Nevertheless, the determination of the daily retention of energy by growing animals is a necessary step in any accurate system of expressing the nutritive requirements of such animals.

It seems a logical extension of Armsby's system to take the daily retention of protein and mineral matter as a scientific measure of the needs of growing animals for these nutrients, even tho Armsby himself did not extend his energy conceptions in this manner. It is perhaps no idle hope that some day it will be possible to express the net protein value of feeds for growth in a manner quite analogous to the expression of their net energy values. Less optimism must be felt that the mineral values of feeds can ever be so simply expressed.

The calculation of the daily retention of nutrients by White Plymouth Rock birds evidently depends upon two determinations: first, the determination of the composition of successive gains in weight; and second, the determination of the rate of gain in weight at different ages. The results of the former determination have already been considered. The latter determination must evidently depend upon the data given in Table 1. However, there is the same objection to using the original observations contained in this table as there was to the use of the experimental results contained in Table 32. This objection rests in the fact that experimental observations upon animals are subject to a considerable variation produced by casual factors, related either to the animal or to its environment, that cannot be brought under experimental control. These casual variations render uncertain to some degree the significance of any single experimental observation. In removing this type of variation as it relates to the data on the composition of the birds at increasing live weights, given in Table 32, the method used was to fit a mathematical curve to the experimental data. The same method will be used in smoothing out the growth observations on the entire flock of White Plymouth Rock birds.

The mathematical procedure, however, is not so simple in this case, because the growth data are not so readily represented by a simple mathematical equation as were the chemical data. It has been previously pointed out that the rate of growth of the birds exhibited a more or less periodical fluctuation. The first point to settle, therefore, in smoothing off the data, is whether these periodical fluctuations are entirely casual in so far as they relate simply to uncontrolled environmental factors, or whether they are related to the growth of White Plymouth Rock birds regardless of environmental changes. The authors have already expressed a hesitancy in attaching any great significance to these fluctuations, because they cannot be interpreted either one way or the other with any degree of assurance, since it is an undoubted fact that weather conditions show a periodical variation.

The belief that uncontrolled environmental factors may entirely account for the apparent cyclic property of the growth curve of White Plymouth Rock birds is strengthened by a comparison of the Illinois data with those obtained at the Purdue Agricultural Experiment Station, to which reference has already been made. In Figs. 8 and 9 such a comparison is made graphically. In these charts the successive biweekly gains in weight expressed in grams are represented by rectangles of proportionate size. In the case of the Illinois data two successive biweekly gains have occasionally been combined in an attempt to smooth out some particularly irregular variation in the rate of growth. The Purdue data have been interpreted by Kempster and Henderson[11] as indicating the existence of two cycles of growth. This interpretation is illustrated by the curve roughly drawn thru the tops of the rectangles in the different sections of Fig. 9. These curves have been patterned as closely as possible after the curves drawn by the above mentioned authors in illustrating their conclusion. On the other hand, the Illinois data obviously cannot be considered as supporting any theory that the growth of White Plymouth Rock birds exhibits only two cycles. The growth obtained may, in fact, be better represented by an assumption of three cycles, as illustrated by the irregular curves drawn thru the tops of the rectangles in Fig. 8.

The marked discrepancy between these two sets of growth data obtained on birds of the same breed may be taken to indicate that the cycles of growth observed are more probably related to periodical variations in environmental factors than to periodical variations in the growth impulse itself. It was decided, therefore, to smooth off the growth data without regard to these periodical fluctuations in the rate of growth. The growth curve of both the Illinois and Purdue flocks is generally of an elongated S type, but unfortunately it cannot be represented thruout its entire range by the S type curve used by Robertson[12], i.e., $\log \dfrac{x}{A-x} = K\,(t-t_1)$ in which x is the growth accomplished at any time, t, A is a constant equal to the maximum value of x, and t_1 is a constant equal to t when x equals one-half A. When this equation is fitted to the entire growth data of either investigation, a very poor fit results for ages of 12 weeks or less. The expedient finally used in overcoming this error, therefore, was to fit the above equation first, to the first 10 or 12 weeks of growth, and second, to the growth subsequent to this period. The equations obtained by this procedure and a graphical presentation of the closeness of fit secured are contained in Figs. 10 and 11. The junction of the two curves for each

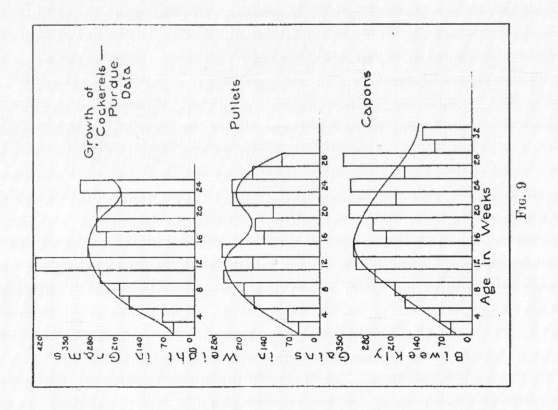

Fig. 9

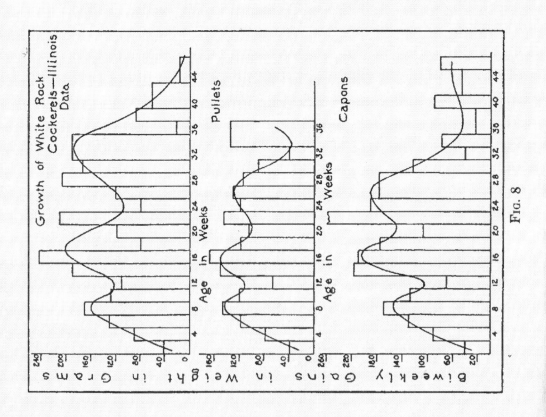

Fig. 8

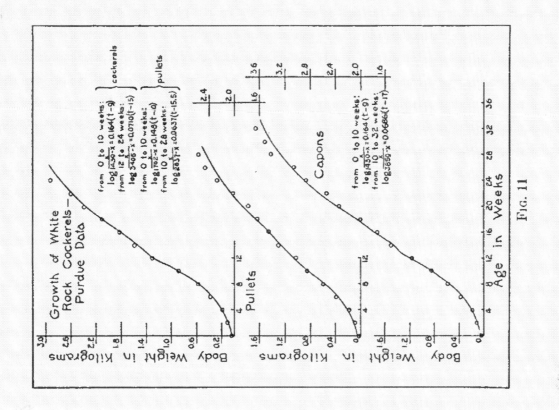

FIG. 11

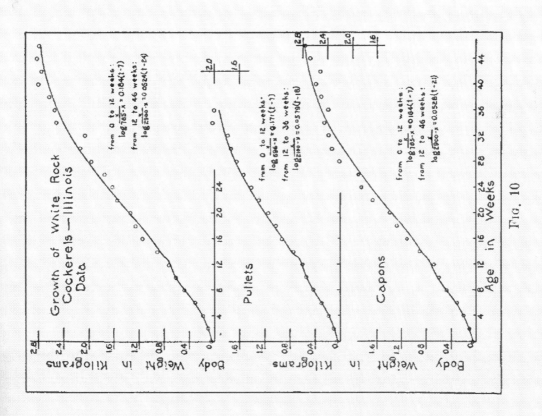

FIG. 10

set of data has no mathematical significance. The use of Robertson's growth curve in this way obviously is purely empirical.

The equations obtained in this manner have been used in estimating the ages at which even pound weights are attained by White Plymouth Rock birds according to the Illinois and the Purdue data. The results thus secured are given in Table 37. The average time required to make successive pound gains in weight have been computed from the data in Table 37 and compiled in Table 38.

From the data shown in Table 35, i. e., the composition of successive pound gains in weight, and in Table 38, the average time required to make successive pound gains in weight, the daily retention of protein, ash, and energy has been computed.[a] Table 39 contains these results. In applying the results of the computed composition of successive gains in weight to the Purdue growth data, the assumption is made that the composition of a bird at a given weight is not appreciably dependent on the time required to reach that weight; in other words, that it is largely independent of the age of the bird. This assumption is, of course, only approximately true. However, the results obtained in this experiment bear out this assumption, particularly the close agreement in composition between the two groups of 1-pound birds killed two weeks apart. It must be admitted, however, that the results in Table 39 based upon the Illinois growth data are open to the criticism that the growth secured was apparently subnormal, while the results based on the Purdue data are open to the criticism that the assumption just considered has not been firmly established, especially for birds of the same weight but differing widely in age.

The abnormally large daily retention of protein, ash, and energy for cockerels weighing 2.5 pounds, indicated by a computation based upon the Purdue growth data, may be explained from the fact that in the Purdue experiment the cockerels and pullets were not separated until the tenth week of age. The Illinois growth data indicate that

---

[a]Obviously, in computing the average daily retention of nutrients up to 1 pound in weight, the composition of the gain from 0 to 1 pound, as given in Table 35, must be corrected for the composition of the bird at hatching. Assuming the hatching weight of White Plymouth Rock birds to be 38 grams, based upon the Purdue data, their composition in grams may be computed by means of the parabolic equations deduced from our own chemical data, with the following results:

	Dry matter	Crude protein	Crude fat	Ash	Gross energy
Calculated	10.56	6.83	1.97	1.10	47
Observed	9.46	6.15	2.13	0.70	56

The observed values given in this tabulation are computed from the average composition of 5 White Rock chicks averaging 1½ days in age (Table 32). The calculated daily retention of nutrients of .5-pound chicks is therefore based upon the estimated composition of 1-pound chicks minus this estimate of the composition of chicks shortly after hatching.

TABLE 37.—AVERAGE AGES AT WHICH EVEN POUND WEIGHTS ARE REACHED BY WHITE PLYMOUTH ROCK BIRDS

Weights	Illinois data			Purdue data		
	Cockerels	Pullets	Capons	Cockerels	Pullets	Capons
lbs.	days	days	days	days	days	days
1...............	54	60	...	49[a]	49[a]	...
2...............	101	112	102	73[a]	73[a]	...
3...............	140	158	140	88	105	92
4...............	177	223	177	111	135	114
5...............	221	...	221	135	175	135
6...............	305	...	304	164	260	158
7...............	...	...	...	...	...	187
8...............	...	...	...	...	...	242

[a]The cockerels and pullets were not separated in the Purdue experiment until the tenth week.

cockerels grow faster than pullets even in the earlier weeks of life, so that the abnormally rapid gain apparently put on by the Purdue cockerels in the period immediately succeeding their separation from the pullets is probably a great exaggeration of the actual gain.

The daily retention of protein by growing cockerels averages a little over 2 grams according to the Illinois growth data, and about twice as much according to the Purdue growth data. The daily retention of mineral matter varies from .2 to .5 gram in one series, and from .3 to about 1 gram in the other. The daily retention of energy increases in both sets of data from 10 to 12 calories to 27 calories in the Illinois estimates, and to 44 calories according to the Purdue estimates (neglecting the abnormal figure for the 2.5-pound birds); after which a decrease in the rate of retention occurs according to the Illinois growth data. The Purdue growth data indicate a sustained maximum retention.

For the pullets and capons a slightly smaller daily retention of protein and mineral matter is indicated than for the cockerels. Altho

TABLE 38.—AVERAGE TIME REQUIRED BY WHITE PLYMOUTH ROCK BIRDS TO MAKE SUCCESSIVE POUND GAINS IN WEIGHT

Gains	Illinois data			Purdue data		
	Cockerels	Pullets	Capons	Cockerels	Pullets	Capons
lbs.	days	days	days	days	days	days
Hatching to 1.....	54	60	...	49	49	...
1 to 2.............	47	52	...	24	24	...
2 to 3.............	39	46	38	15	32	19
3 to 4.............	37	65	37	23	30	22
4 to 5.............	44	...	44	24	40	21
5 to 6.............	84	...	83	29	85	23
6 to 7.............	...	...	...	...	...	29
7 to 8.............	...	...	...	...	...	55

the gains on the pullets, especially at the higher weights, contained more energy than the gains on the cockerels, this is almost exactly offset by the slower rate at which the pullets grew, so that little consistent difference is evident in the daily retention of energy by cockerels and pullets. The greater energy content of the gains of capons as compared with cockerels is not offset by a slower growth, so that the values in Table 39 indicate a larger daily retention of energy by capons than by cockerels of like weight.

TABLE 39.—DAILY RETENTION OF PROTEIN, ASH, AND ENERGY BY WHITE PLYMOUTH ROCK BIRDS OF DIFFERENT WEIGHTS

Kind of bird and weight	Illinois data				Purdue data			
	Age	Protein	Ash	Energy	Age	Protein	Ash	Energy
COCKERELS lbs.	days	gms.	gms.	cals.	days	gms.	gms.	cals.
0.5...............	34	1.42	0.23	10.5	32	1.57	0.26	11.6
1.5...............	89	1.88	0.32	15.9	61	3.68	0.63	31.1
2.5...............	122	2.39	0.43	22.5	75	6.21	1.11	58.5
3.5...............	158	2.65	0.49	27.3	99	4.26	0.79	43.9
4.5...............	197	2.34	0.44	25.9	122	4.28	0.81	47.5
5.5...............	250	1.28	0.25	15.2	148	3.71	0.72	43.9
PULLETS lbs.								
0.5...............	34	1.24	0.21	9.6	32	1.52	0.26	11.8
1.5...............	85	1.69	0.27	17.5	62	3.66	0.59	37.9
2.5...............	132	2.06	0.32	26.0	89	2.96	0.45	37.4
3.5...............	183	1.56	0.23	22.9	120	3.38	0.49	49.5
4.5...............	...	....	....	....	153	2.70	0.38	44.3
5.5...............	...	....	....	....	204	1.35	0.18	24.2
CAPONS lbs.								
2.5...............	120	2.29	0.38	27.0	80	4.59	0.75	54.0
3.5...............	157	2.37	0.37	32.5	103	3.98	0.62	54.7
4.5...............	195	2.00	0.29	31.4	124	4.20	0.61	65.8
5.5...............	249	1.07	0.15	18.8	146	3.86	0.53	67.8
6.5...............	...	....	....	....	172	3.08	0.39	59.9
7.5...............	...	....	....	....	209	1.63	0.19	34.8

It is of interest to compare the rate of retention of protein by growing White Plymouth Rock chickens with the rate of retention of protein by other species of farm animals. Armsby[13] has made an extensive compilation of such data for cattle, sheep, and swine, and has found that when the daily retention is expressed in terms of gain of protein per 1,000 pounds live weight per day, the change in rate of retention is fairly well represented by the equation, $g = \dfrac{135}{a + 20}$; in which g is the gain of protein in pounds per day per 1,000 pounds live weight, and a is the age in days. This equation corresponds fairly well with the general average of the observed results on cattle and sheep, especially for the later ages. With swine the few results available appear to indicate a greater rate of protein retention during the first three months than would be predicted from this equation.

A comparison of the daily retention of protein per pound of live weight calculated from this equation, with the daily retention of pro-

TABLE 40.—CALCULATED AND OBSERVED DAILY RETENTION OF PROTEIN PER POUND LIVE WEIGHT BY WHITE PLYMOUTH ROCK COCKERELS

| Body weight | Illinois data | | | Purdue data | | |
| | Protein retention per day per pound body weight | | | Protein retention per day per pound body weight | | |
	Age	Observed	Calculated[a]	Age	Observed	Calculated[a]
lbs.	days	gms.	gms.	days	gms.	gms.
0.5	34	2.84	1.13	32	3.14	1.18
1.5	89	1.25	0.56	61	2.45	0.76
2.5	122	0.96	0.43	75	2.48	0.64
3.5	158	0.76	0.34	99	1.22	0.52
4.5	197	0.52	0.28	122	0.95	0.43
5.5	250	0.23	0.21	148	0.68	0.36

[a]The estimated protein retention was calculated by the use of Armsby's generalized equation given on page 378 of "The Nutrition of Farm Animals."

tein as computed from the Illinois analyses and growth data on White Plymouth Rocks, and also from the growth data reported from Purdue, appears in Table 40. The rate of gain of protein by growing White Plymouth Rock cockerels is two to three times as rapid as that predicted from Armsby's equation deduced from data for larger farm animals.

A comparison of the rate of gain of energy by White Plymouth Rock cockerels and by growing calves may be made using Armsby's estimates of the rate of gain of energy per day and per

TABLE 41.—ESTIMATED RATE OF GAIN OF ENERGY PER DAY PER POUND LIVE WEIGHT OF WHITE PLYMOUTH ROCK COCKERELS AS COMPARED WITH ARMSBY'S SIMILAR ESTIMATES FOR CALVES OF LIKE AGES

| Illinois data | | | Purdue data | | |
| Energy retained daily per pound live weight | | | Energy retained daily per pound live weight | | |
Age	Cockerels	Calves[a]	Age	Cockerels	Calves[a]
days	cals.	cals.	days	cals.	cals.
34	21.0	17.4	32	23.2	17.6
89	10.6	11.1	61	20.7	13.4
122	9.0	8.9	75	23.4	12.2
158	7.8	7.1	99	12.5	10.4
197	5.8	5.6	122	10.5	8.9
250	2.8	5.0	148	8.0	7.6

[a]The estimates for calves were obtained by simple interpolation from Table 94, page 402, of Armsby's "The Nutrition of Farm Animals."

1,000 pounds live weight by calves of different ages.[14] While Armsby also estimates the rate of gain of energy by swine, his estimates can-not be considered reliable, because of the small amount of data upon which they are based and because of discrepancies existing among them.

In Table 41 the rate of gain of energy made by White Plymouth Rock cockerels, per pound of live weight, at increasing ages, is compared with Armsby's estimated rates of gain of energy by calves per pound of live weight. The estimates for calves included in each comparison have been obtained from Armsby's Table 94 by simple interpolation. Except for the earliest and the latest age, a remark-ably close agreement exists between the estimated rate of gain of en-ergy of White Plymouth Rock cockerels computed from the Illinois growth data and the estimated rate of gain of energy by calves of equal age. For the estimates based upon the Purdue growth data no close agreement exists with Armsby's estimates at equal ages.

SUMMARY AND CONCLUSIONS

An investigation of the growth of White Plymouth Rock chick-ens was made, involving observations of the increase in live weight, the increase in body measurements, the increase in weight of individ-ual organs and parts of the carcass, and the changing chemical compo-sition of the carcass and of gains in weight with increase in size.

The growth and body weight of a flock of White Plymouth Rock chickens numbering approximately 1,000 at the beginning of the ex-periment was determined by weighing the birds individually every two weeks. The growth of cockerels and pullets was observed sep-arately as soon as the sex could be distinguished. When the cockerels reached an age of 10 weeks, approximately half of them were capon-ized, and from this time constituted a third group of birds. The rate of growth as measured by the biweekly increase in body weight was found to vary periodically. These variations, however, have not been interpreted as representing true cycles of growth, because it is believed that they more probably are related to periodical variations in en-vironmental conditions, particularly variations in the weather.

Relative Growth of Cockerels, Capons, and Pullets.—The growth of the cockerels proceeded at a distinctly more rapid rate than that of the pullets, even from the time when the separation was first made. The rate of growth of the capons was not distinctly different from that of the cockerels up to a weight of approximately 6 pounds. All groups of birds grew at a much slower rate than the Purdue flock reported upon in Bulletin 214 from that station.

From a study of the change in the ten body measurements with advancing age, it appears that practically all of the measurements in-creased in approximately the same proportion when referred to the measurements of the .5-pound chicks. Thus, for the cockerels, all the measurements except the length of middle toe increased approximately two and a half times from the .5-pound to the 7-pound weight. This would appear to mean that the conformation of the birds did not change materially during the whole course of growth between these two extreme weights.

At equal weights the pullets were, in general, smaller in external measurement than the cockerels, the only measurement remaining approximately the same in the two sexes being the length of keel. The leg measurements of the pullets in particular were appreciably smaller than those of the cockerels of like weight, especially after a weight of 3 pounds was reached.

On the other hand, no distinct differences between the body measurements of capons and cockerels at equal weights were revealed. Castration apparently does not appreciably affect the body shape of White Plymouth Rock cockerels.

Estimating Surface Area.—The surface area of all birds slaughtered in this experiment was directly determined by measuring the area of the skin after removal from the carcass. In attempting to find a formula by which the body surface of White Plymouth Rock chickens could be estimated readily, it was found that the Meeh formula could not be used over the entire range of weight from .5 to 7 pounds. However, the Meeh formula may be applied with considerable accuracy to birds weighing more than 1 pound, using the value of 9.85 for the constant, the area being expressed in square centimeters and the weight in grams. A slightly more accurate formula, which may be used for birds weighing from 1 to 7 pounds, inclusive, was devised by the use of one of the body measurements, namely, the rump-to-shoulder measurement, along with the body weight. This formula is as follows:

$$S = 5.86 \ W^{.5} \ L^{.6}$$

in which S is the surface area in square centimeters, W, the weight in grams, and L, the rump-to-shoulder distance in centimeters. This formula also applies to Rhode Island Red chickens, but evidently does not apply to White Leghorns unless the constant is made smaller (i.e., 5.03).

Growth of Different Parts of Carcass and Viscera.—From a study of the weights of the different organs and the different parts of the carcass, it is evident that most of these increase in weight continuously with advancing age. The digestive organs, however, are somewhat exceptional in their growth, since they reach their maximum size before the bird has obtained its complete growth.

The offal part of the carcass, not including the inedible viscera, was found to constitute a fairly constant percentage of the empty weight of the birds at all weights, namely, very close to 19 percent. This constancy in percentage weight holds particularly for the blood weights. The percentage weight of blood is consistently higher for the cockerels than for the pullets. The capons occupy an intermediate position in this respect.

Following an initial increase from the .5-pound to the 1-pound chicks, the percentage weight of the total viscera showed a continuous decrease with increasing weight of birds. This conforms with similar data on man and other mammals.

The percentage weight of the total dressed carcass increased slightly, but continuously, with increasing empty weight of the bird. This relative increase in dressed carcass relates more to the muscular tissue than to the bones. For all three groups of birds the percentage weight of bone in the dressed carcass decreased with increasing body weight, while the percentage weight of flesh and fat increased.

The total weights of offal were consistently less for the pullets than for the cockerels of like weight. This is true of each item in the offal, except the feathers. The weights of feathers for the pullets were generally greater than those for the cockerels. While the total weights of viscera did not differ greatly for cockerels and pullets, some apparently significant differences existed between the two sexes relative to individual organs. For example, at a weight of 2 pounds the lungs of the pullets weighed the same as the lungs of the cockerels, but with increasing body weight the lungs of the cockerels weighed more than those of the pullets, the differences increasing with increasing body weight. Just the reverse is true with the kidneys. The weights of spleen were consistently heavier for the pullets than for the cockerels. The dressed carcass in the pullets was always slightly heavier than in the cockerels for body weights of 3 pounds or more, altho the weights of bone in the dressed carcass were always greater at the same body weight for cockerels than for pullets. In other words, the edible flesh and fat always constituted a greater percentage of the empty weight of the pullets than of the cockerels of equal weight.

Differences between cockerels and capons relative to the weights of the different parts of the body were not so numerous nor so consistent as those between cockerels and pullets. However, at a weight of 7 pounds some interesting differences apparently existed. The heart weights were distinctly greater for the cockerels than for the capons at this weight, while the weights of liver, kidney, spleen, and intestines for the capons were distinctly greater than for the cockerels. The average weights of kidney and spleen were greater for the capons than for the cockerels at all weights. Apparently castration profoundly affected the growth of these visceral organs.

Chemical Composition of Birds.—The data relating to the chemical composition of the birds showed the changes in dry matter, protein, ash, fat, and energy with increasing age that would be expected from similar studies on other animals. Comparing the three groups of birds, the analyses show that the pullets fattened distinctly more rapidly than the cockerels, while the capons occupied an intermediate position. The energy values per gram of tissue for the pullets for weights above 3 pounds were always distinctly higher than the energy values for either cockerels or capons. The energy values of all samples obtained in this experiment were directly determined by means of the bomb calorimeter.

The distribution of nutrients between the three composite samples analyzed in this experiment,—namely, (1) the flesh and edible viscera, (2) the bones of the dressed carcass, and (3) the head, shanks and feet, blood, feathers, and non-edible viscera (conveniently referred to as the offal),—did not show any progressive changes with advancing age. The flesh and edible viscera contained on an average 35.5 percent of the total dry matter, 40.8 percent of the total protein, 30.2 percent of the total fat, 37.2 percent of the total gross energy, and 14.7 percent of the total ash of the entire carcass.

At equal live weights, pullets contained more edible fat and energy and as much edible protein as cockerels, the difference with respect to fat and energy increasing rapidly with increasing live weight. Capons, at equal weights, contained amounts of edible fat and energy midway between cockerels and pullets, and smaller amounts of edible protein than either.

From the analysis of these three composite samples the composition of the live birds at the different weights was computed, and from these figures, the weights of chemical constituents contained in birds weighing exactly 0.5, 1.0, 1.5, 2.0, 3.0 pounds, etc. To render more accurate the subsequent calculations of the composition of successive pound gains in weight, the experimental data on the composition of birds at definite weights were smoothed out by fitting to them parabolic equations of the general type,

$$y = ax + bx^2$$

the constants being determined by the method of least squares. From the equations thus obtained the composition of birds at even pound weights was estimated, and from these estimations the composition of successive pound gains in weight was determined.

Rate of Retention of Nutrients During Growth.—In computing the daily retention of nutrients by birds of different ages, the data on the corrected composition of successive gains and the data on the growth and body weight of the entire flock of birds were used. The latter were also smoothed out by mathematical means in a purely empirical fashion. Since, however, the growth of the flock of birds used in this experiment was considerably slower than the growth of White Plymouth Rock chickens reported from the Purdue Experiment Station by Philips, two sets of values on the daily retention of nutrients were computed, applying the values on the composition of successive gains to both the Illinois and the Purdue corrected growth data.

The daily retention of protein by White Plymouth Rock cockerels evidently ranges between 2 grams and 4.5 grams per day, depending upon whether they are growing at their maximum rate or at a slower and probably more nearly average rate for birds on the farm. Except for smaller figures for the first two months of growth and a slowing up of growth as maturity is approached, no marked change in the daily retention of protein at increasing ages was noted. The daily retention of protein by pullets and capons was less than that for cockerels. The daily retention of mineral matter by White Plymouth Rock cockerels ranges between .2 gram and 1 gram per head, with no clear progressive variation except for the early ages up to a weight of 2.5 pounds. The maximum retention of mineral matter was established at a level of .5 to .8 gram daily. The daily retention of minerals by pullets and capons appeared to be distinctly less than that by cockerels.

The estimates of the daily retention of energy by growing cockerels were quite variable at different ages, showing no progressive changes after a weight of 2.5 pounds was reached. The average daily rate of gain of energy from 2.5 pounds upward was about 25 calories according to the Illinois growth data, and about 45 to 50 calories according to the Purdue growth data.

Between pullets and cockerels no differences in the rate of retention of energy were apparent, tho for capons, the daily retention of energy was consistently higher than for cockerels.

LITERATURE CITED

1. ARMSBY, H. P. The nutrition of farm animals, p. 400. Macmillan. 1917.
2. PURDUE AGR. EXP. STA. Bul. 214.
3. HOGAN, A. G., and SKOUBY, C. I. Journ. Agr. Res. 25, 419-430. 1923.
4. JACKSON, C. M. Amer. Journ. Anat. 15, 1. 1913-14.
5. DONALDSON, H. H. Amer. Jour. Physiol. 67, 1. 1923-24.
6. DONALDSON, H. H. Trans. 15th Internatl. Cong. Hyg. and Démog. Washington, D. C. 1912.
7. MARRASSINI, A., and LUCIANI, L. Arch. Ital. Biol. 56, 395. 1911-12.
8. HATAI, S. Anat. Rec. 9, 647. 1915.
9. HOSKINS, R. G. Amer. Jour. Physiol. 72, 324. 1925.
10. RICHTER, C. P. Johns Hopkins Hosp. Rpts. 36, 324. 1925.
11. KEMPSTER, H. L., and HENDERSON, E. W. Normal growth of domestic animals. Mo. Agr. Exp. Sta. Res. Bul. 62, 40. 1923.
12. ROBERTSON, T. B. The chemical basis of growth and senescence. Lippincott. 1923.
13. ARMSBY, H. P. The nutrition of farm animals, p. 378. Macmillan. 1917.
14. ARMSBY, H. P. The nutrition of farm animals, p. 402. Macmillan. 1917.

Appendix Table 1.—Average Live Weight, Average Weight of Contents of Alimentary Tract, Average Weight of Empty Bird, and Average Weight of Bird by Summation of Samples

Kind of bird and weight	Average live weight	Average weight of contents of alimentary tract	Contents as percentage of live bird	Average weight of empty bird	Weight by summation of samples	Difference	
	gms.	gms.	perct.	gms.	gms.	gms.	perct.
COCKERELS							
lbs.							
0.5	232	16	6.9	216	191	25	11.6
1	447	30	6.7	417	402	15	3.6
1	452	23	5.1	429	412	17	4.0
1.5	673	36	5.4	637	612	25	3.9
2	993	27	2.7	967	917	50	5.2
3	1 361	56	4.1	1 305	1 258	47	3.6
4	1 786	61	3.4	1 725	1 658	67	3.9
5	2 236	80	3.6	2 156	2 106	50	2.3
6	2 583	74	2.9	2 509	2 425	84	3.3
7	3 253	74	2.3	3 180	3 076	104	3.3
PULLETS							
lbs.							
2	961	50	5.7	911	869	42	4.6
3	1 342	49	3.6	1 293	1 256	37	2.9
4	1 842	55	3.0	1 787	1 731	56	3.1
5	2 340	95	4.0	2 245	2 164	81	3.6
CAPONS							
lbs.							
3	1 375	61	4.4	1 315	1 272	43	3.3
4	1 702	47	2.7	1 655	1 605	50	3.0
5	2 285	60	2.6	2 225	2 151	74	3.3
6	2 684	84	3.1	2 600	2 507	93	3.6
7	3 188	96	3.0	3 093	2 983	110	3.6

APPENDIX TABLE 2.—ANALYTICAL DATA ON THE COMPOSITE SAMPLES
(The "total" percentages are based on the average empty weights of the birds.)

No. of chick-ens	Approxi-mate weight	Kind of bird	Sample	Weight	Dry substance		Crude protein (N x 6.0)		Ash		Ether extract		Gross energy	
	lbs.			gms.	perct.	gms.	perct.	gms.	perct.	gms.	perct.	gms.	small cals. per gm.	total therms
5	0.5	Cockerels	Flesh	361	30.07	108.49	20.88	75.34	1.44	5.20	4.38	15.80	1 526	0.55
			Bone	192	39.97	76.66	19.68	37.75	8.81	16.90	4.57	8.77	1 703	0.33
			Offal	402	34.30	137.89	22.25	89.45	2.56	10.29	6.63	26.65	1 762	0.71
			Total	955	29.94	323.01	18.77	202.54	3.00	32.39	4.75	51.22	1 474	1.59
5	1	Cockerels	Flesh	816	25.40	207.16	19.56	159.53	1.27	10.36	3.95	32.22	1 361	1.11
			Bone	351	41.46	145.69	17.40	61.14	11.30	39.71	9.86	34.65	1 978	0.69
			Offal	840	29.74	249.82	21.12	177.41	2.36	19.82	7.67	64.43	1 825	1.53
			Total	2 007	28.92	602.67	19.10	398.08	3.35	69.89	6.30	131.30	1 598	3.33
5	1	Cockerels	Flesh	869	24.87	216.05	19.62	170.44	1.31	11.38	3.55	30.85	1 281	1.11
			Bone	373	39.36	146.62	18.72	69.73	11.23	41.83	6.87	25.59	1 572	0.59
			Offal	816	29.73	242.60	20.20	164.83	2.42	19.75	5.33	43.49	1 601	1.31
			Total	2 058	28.19	605.27	18.86	405.00	3.40	72.96	4.65	99.93	1 404	3.01
5	1.5	Cockerels	Flesh	1 291	28.63	369.61	20.04	258.66	1.27	16.39	6.54	84.41	1 540	1.99
			Bone	545	42.42	231.06	19.20	104.58	12.52	68.20	8.86	48.26	1 810	0.99
			Offal	1 223	33.86	413.20	21.67	264.45	2.37	28.89	9.36	114.21	1 976	2.42
			Total	3 059	31.83	1 013.87	19.70	627.69	3.56	113.48	7.75	246.88	1 695	5.40
5	2	Cockerels	Flesh	1 907	27.20	518.70	18.84	359.28	1.07	20.40	6.16	117.47	1 507	3.05
			Bone	920	44.40	408.48	17.76	163.39	10.34	95.13	14.75	135.70	2 243	2.06
			Offal	1 758	36.21	636.57	21.04	369.88	2.39	42.02	9.88	173.69	2 092	3.68
			Total	4 585	32.36	1 563.75	18.47	892.55	3.26	157.55	8.83	426.86	1 819	8.79
5	3	Cockerels	Flesh	2 756	28.51	785.65	20.10	553.90	1.13	31.14	4.39	120.98	1 571	4.33
			Bone	1 213	45.00	545.72	18.42	223.38	11.19	135.70	11.70	141.89	2 046	2.48
			Offal	2 318	37.64	873.94	24.72	574.06	2.31	53.55	9.72	225.62	(1 385)	3.21a
			Total	6 287	33.80	2 205.31	20.71	1 351.34	3.38	220.39	7.49	488.49	1 533	10.02
5	4	Cockerels	Flesh	3 587	29.49	1 057.75	21.00	753.23	1.02	36.59	3.92	140.60	1 460	5.24
			Bone	1 651	45.26	747.42	19.86	327.97	12.56	207.42	12.20	201.47	2 194	3.62
			Offal	3 054	36.78	1 120.90	24.15	736.13	1.98	60.48	8.77	267.26	2 289	6.99
			Total	8 292	33.92	2 926.07	21.07	1 817.33	3.53	304.49	7.07	609.33	1 838	15.85
5	5	Cockerels	Flesh	4 601	28.49	1 310.91	19.74	908.30	1.29	59.36	5.54	254.91	1 651b	7.60
			Bone	2 012	47.61	957.96	18.54	373.04	14.44	290.55	13.30	267.61	2 273	4.57
			Offal	3 918	41.54	1 630.94	25.62	1 006.13	2.01	78.87	11.13	437.21	2 137	8.39
			Total	10 531	36.17	3 899.81	21.22	2 287.47	3.98	428.78	8.90	959.73	1 908	20.56

aThe calculated energy content of this sample is 5.41 therms, or 2,336 small calories per gram.
bThe energy value obtained on analysis was 2,258, which is obviously incorrect. The value 1,651, calculated by using 5.7 calories and 9.5 calories per gram of protein and fat respectively, is used.

APPENDIX TABLE 2.—Continued

No. of chickens	Approximate weight	Kind of bird	Sample	Weight	Dry substance		Crude protein (N x 6.0)		Ash		Ether extract		Gross energy	
	lbs.			gms.	perct.	gms.	perct.	gms.	perct.	gms.	perct.	gms.	small cals. per gm.	total therms
5	6	Cockerels	Flesh	5 680	28.51	1 619.37	20.22	1 148.50	1.72	97.70	5.40	306.72	1 714	9.74
			Bone	2 089	51.37	1 073.12	18.84	393.57	16.51	344.89	14.47	302.28	2 459	5.14
			Offal	4 354	53.34	2 322.42	34.02	1 481.23	4.13	179.82	13.12	571.24	2 774	12.08
			Total	12 123	39.97	5 014.91	24.09	3 023.30	4.96	622.41	9.41	1 180.24	2 149	26.96
5	7	Cockerels	Flesh	7 577	28.08	2 127.62	21.00	1 591.17	1.40	106.08	4.46	337.93	1 606	12.17
			Bone	2 549	50.77	1 294.13	20.16	513.88	15.73	400.96	12.26	312.51	2 317	5.91
			Offal	5 254	51.69	2 715.79	26.70	1 405.06	2.65	139.45	19.89	1 045.02	3 255	17.10
			Total	15 380	38.61	6 137.54	22.08	3 510.11	4.06	646.49	10.67	1 695.46	2 213	35.18
5	2	Pullets	Flesh	1 888	26.70	504.10	19.02	359.10	1.06	20.01	6.00	113.28	1 515	2.86
			Bone	808	45.40	366.83	18.18	146.89	11.35	91.71	13.57	109.65	2 145	1.73
			Offal	1 650	40.08	661.32	24.16	398.64	2.49	41.09	11.86	195.69	2 094	3.46
			Total	4 346	33.62	1 532.25	19.85	904.63	3.35	152.81	9.19	418.62	1 765	8.05
5	3	Pullets	Flesh	2 859	34.09	974.77	18.90	540.43	1.20	34.31	9.75	278.79	1 860	5.32
			Bone	1 119	44.35	496.05	18.00	201.33	10.07	112.63	13.57	151.78	2 185	2.45
			Offal	2 303	37.86c	871.92	24.22c	557.79	2.59	59.65	10.35c	238.36	2 364d	5.44
			Total	6 281	36.24	2 342.74	20.10	1 299.55	3.19	206.59	10.35	668.93	2 042	13.21
5	4	Pullets	Flesh	4 146	30.79	1 276.46	18.54	768.61	1.01	41.87	11.22	465.15	2 262	9.38
			Bone	1 339	51.86	694.51	17.76	237.84	12.70	170.08	18.30	245.07	2 505	3.35
			Offal	3 169	49.94	1 581.98	25.83	818.27	1.89	60.00	19.14	606.30	2 758	8.74
			Total	8 654	39.76	3 552.95	20.42	1 824.72	3.04	271.95	13.61	1 316.52	2 401	21.47
5	5	Pulletss	Flesh	5 270	33.67	1 774.41	20.22	1 065.59	1.35	71.15	12.62	665.07	2 356	12.42
			Bone	1 658	54.87	909.74	18.78	311.37	14.30	237.09	20.00	331.6c	2 955	4.90
			Offal	3 892	31.86	2 018.39	27.71	1 078.47	1.82	70.83	23.07	897.88	3 516	13.68
			Total	10 820	41.90	4 702.54	21.88	2 455.43	3.38	379.07	16.88	1 894.5	2 762	31.00

cCalculated from average percentage composition of offal from 3-pound capons and cockerels. This sample was accidentally thrown out before analysis.
dCalculated using factors of 5.7 calories per gram of protein and 9.5 calories per gram of fat.

Appendix Table 2.—Concluded

No. of chickens	Approximate weight	Kind of bird	Sample	Weight	Dry substance		Crude protein (N x 6.0)		Ash		Ether extract		Gross energy	
	lbs.			gms.	perct.	gms.	perct.	gms.	perct.	gms.	perct.	gms.	small cals. per gm.	total therms
5	3	Capons	Flesh	2 832	28.20	798.62	19.74	559.04	1.27	35.97	5.99	169.64	1 628	4.61
			Bone	1 186	44.40	526.58	18.30	217.04	10.84	128.56	13.40	158.92	2 223	2.64
			Offal	2 341	38.08	889.10	23.72	553.86	2.60	60.67	10.98	256.27	2 280	5.34
			Total	6 359	33.68	2 214.30	20.23	1 329.94	3.42	225.20	8.90	584.83	1 916	12.59
5	4	Capons	Flesh	3 365	29.25	984.26	19.26	648.10	1.11	37.35	7.16	240.93	1 787	6.01
			Bone	1 595	46.75	745.57	18.24	290.89	11.82	188.51	13.54	215.94	2 491	3.97
			Offal	3 066	40.65	1 247.66	24.12	740.33	2.02	61.98	12.12	371.89	2 736	8.39
			Total	8 026	35.98	2 977.49	20.30	1 679.32	3.47	287.84	10.02	828.76	2 217	18.37
5	5	Capons	Flesh	4 642	33.10	1 536.50	19.38	809.58	1.17	54.31	8.61	399.66	1 893	8.79
			Bone	2 061	48.12	991.56	18.72	385.74	11.57	238.41	16.15	332.79	2 628	5.42
			Offal	4 052	42.18	1 710.82	22.29	903.98	1.85	74.92	14.86	602.66	2 803	11.36
			Total	10 755	38.11	4 238.88	19.68	2 189.30	3.30	367.64	12.00	1 335.11	2 297	25.57
5	6	Capons	Flesh	5 745	31.43	1 805.65	18.84	1 082.36	0.98	56.30	10.29	591.16	2 049	11.77
			Bone	2 200	50.76	1 116.72	18.84	414.48	14.65	322.30	15.33	337.26	2 597	5.71
			Offal	4 592	54.18	2 485.75	29.45	1 351.36	2.34	107.31	18.99	871.43	3 120	14.33
			Total	12 537	41.76	5 408.12	21.99	2 848.20	3.75	485.91	13.90	1 799.85	2 456	31.81
5	7	Capons	Flesh	7 412	36.97	2 740.22	18.00	1 334.16	0.94	69.67	16.84	1 248.18	2 543	18.85
			Bone	2 455	52.95	1 299.92	17.34	425.70	11.86	291.16	21.68	532.24	2 919	7.17
			Offal	5 048	51.37	2 495.22	25.85	1 305.29	2.22	111.92	20.87	1 053.79	3 396	17.14
			Total	14 915	42.90	6 634.36	19.82	3 065.15	3.06	472.75	18.33	2 834.21	2 790	43.16

40926739R00040